THE YEAR EVERYTHING COLLIDED

BRYAN JONES

(CODE NAME: GENESIS™)

TABLE OF CONTENTS

THE YEAR EVERYTHING COLLIDED

Inside the Most Important Year of the Modern Age

By the closing months of 2025, it was obvious—at least to anyone paying quiet, honest attention—that something far larger than "normal turbulence" was unfolding across the surface of everyday life. It did not arrive as a single headline that froze the feeds or a single catastrophe that carved the year into "before" and "after." It arrived as repetition. As a pattern. As the same uneasy rhythm echoing through different nations, different industries, different households, different nervous systems, all humming with a shared sense that something fundamental was out of alignment.

You could see it under fluorescent lights in ordinary grocery stores, where prices behaved less like numbers and more like rumors—restless, jumpy, and strangely detached from the calm explanations offered by officials who spoke of "temporary pressures" and "manageable inflation" while families rearranged items at the register because the total quietly crossed another invisible line.

You could feel it in workplaces that had once sold themselves as "careers" but now felt like extended holding patterns. People showed up to meetings with carefully rehearsed enthusiasm while, on a second screen or a late-night browser tab, they sketched escape routes: half-formed business ideas, job applications never finished, relocation searches that ended in an open map and a tired sigh. They did not yet have the money or clarity to leave, but they no longer believed they were staying by choice.

You could hear it in classrooms, hospitals, freight yards, call centers, and public offices, where professionals who had once wrapped their identity around the nobility of their roles now described their days as "managing fallout" or "putting out fires," as if their work had shifted from building a future to sweeping up the fragments of one. Their language was still professional. Their eyes were not.

Governments told their citizens that the situation was under control— that supply chains were "stabilizing," that conflicts were "contained," that currencies were "resilient," that institutions were "strong."

Markets framed every sharp movement as a temporary correction in an otherwise healthy system—a little volatility, a short-term overreaction, a buying opportunity.

Technology firms unveiled the next generation of tools that would, according to their own marketing, save time, save labor, save attention, save the planet—while quietly feeding on all four.

And yet, beneath the noise of press conferences, earnings calls, and launch events, an unspoken recognition began to spread like a low-frequency signal through the collective nervous system:

the story we had been telling ourselves about how the world works no longer fit the facts in front of us.

The first instinct, as always, was to shrink the problem down to something familiar enough to argue about.

For some, the villain was politics—too polarized, too corrupt, too captured by donors, lobbyists, and ideological performance.

For others, the culprit was economics—too unequal, too financialized, too dependent on abstractions like derivatives and debt ceilings and "liquidity injections" that most people could not visualize, let alone influence.

Others pointed to technology—too invasive, too fast, too entangled with attention, labor, and identity to be treated as a neutral tool.

Culture, religion, globalization, demographic change, climate instability, generational resentment—each became a convenient container for blame, a way to attach dread to something with a clear label and a familiar enemy.

None of these explanations were completely wrong.

They were simply not enough.

They treated symptoms as origins, mistook downstream dysfunctions for upstream causes, and framed each crisis as an isolated malfunction instead of a coordinated expression of a deeper structural shift.

From a wider vantage point, another picture came into focus. What emerged was not a chaotic collage of unrelated problems, but a single accelerating arc: a world that had been moving toward a convergence point for decades, layering pressure upon pressure, abstraction upon abstraction, speed upon speed, until the weight of its own design began to exceed the capacity of its systems—and its people—to carry it.

By 2025, we were close enough to that convergence to feel its gravity.

The year 2026 did not *create* that convergence.

It exposed it.

To say "the world broke in 2026" is to misunderstand what actually occurred. The fracture was already present—threaded through supply chains optimized for efficiency instead of resilience, through political systems that relied on permanent outrage to mobilize voters, through digital platforms that monetized attention by fragmenting it, through social contracts that promised stability while quietly offloading risk onto individuals, through the human psyche itself, stretched thin by a decade of always-on everything.

For years, language and spectacle and routine had functioned as a global anesthetic, numbing societies to the depth of their own instability. We called disruption "the new normal," as if naming the agitation were enough to domesticate it. The turning point arrived not when chaos appeared, but when the illusions designed to conceal that chaos could no longer hold their shape.

Throughout 2025, the evidence accumulated in plain sight for anyone willing to observe without flinching. Volatility that had once been described as "temporary turbulence" started to look suspiciously like baseline behavior. What used to be called "once-in-a-century" events seemed to arrive with the frequency of software updates. Conflicts that were framed as regional disputes reconfigured energy prices, trade routes, migration patterns, and elections far beyond their borders. A drone strike in one time zone translated into higher fuel costs in another; a cyberattack on a distant grid rippled into hospital delays and factory shutdowns continents away.

Technologies introduced as tools of convenience quietly rewrote the structure of labor, the architecture of attention, and even the definition of identity at a speed that laws, schools, and cultural norms were not built to match. Artificial intelligence leapt from speculative buzzword to everyday infrastructure in months, not decades. What had been dismissed as "assistive" capabilities suddenly encroached on creative, analytical, and relational work that many people had believed would be protected by their education or talent.

The crucial shift was not merely quantitative—more crises, more headlines, more disruptions. It was qualitative.

The world was no longer just unstable.

It was compressed.

Military, financial, political, ecological, cultural, and psychological pressures all intensified and synchronized inside an interconnected system with almost no slack. Shock in one node was transmitted almost instantly to all the others. A blockage at a single port, a regulatory change around one currency, a rogue line of code in one critical system could alter the trajectories of millions of lives in ways no one had explicitly chosen. There was no true "elsewhere" left to absorb impact.

This is what I mean by collision.

Collision is not only the spectacular image of impact—the war broadcast live, the market crash plotted on a graph, the viral video that detonates across platforms, the scandal, the outage, the blackout. Collision is what happens when long-running trajectories that were assumed to be separate—economic growth, technological progress, political polarization, environmental strain, psychological overload—turn out to be convergent, and their combined force exceeds the capacity of existing systems to absorb them.

It is the moment when patterns that were easy to dismiss as anomalies reveal themselves as the main story.

By that definition, 2026 was not just another year.

It was a junction.

A crossing where war and code, identity and debt, surveillance and escapism, fear and power all intersected at scale. It was the year when older tools for managing risk—diplomacy, regulation, monetary adjustments, public messaging, even traditional forms of protest and civic engagement—proved insufficient on their own. The world did not simply feel unstable; it felt electrically charged, as if every domain of life had been wired into the same overloaded circuit and someone kept turning up the current.

Decades of digital connectivity had woven distant events into a single fabric of cause and effect. A policy tweak in one capital could shift job prospects in a city that had never appeared on that policymaker's radar. A miscalculation in a contested region could redraw supply chains, housing markets, and domestic politics across oceans. An algorithmic adjustment to what people saw when they unlocked their phones could subtly alter the emotional climate of entire populations by breakfast.

Locality, as a protective concept, eroded. Everything fed into everything else.

As this cascading interdependence tightened, ordinary language began to fail. Words like "crisis," "emergency," and "uncertainty" were invoked so often, and with so little precision, that they lost their sharpness. Public discourse swung wildly between sensationalism and sedation—between "everything is collapsing right now" and "everything is basically fine if you stop overreacting"—leaving little space for sustained, clear-eyed analysis. People were not only misinformed. They were saturated. Overbriefed and underoriented.

And yet, beneath the confusion, another possibility remained.

Even in a system organized around distraction, the human capacity for sustained observation had not disappeared. Even in a culture that rewarded hot takes and punished nuance, it was still possible for an individual to step half a pace back from the noise and actually look. Not everyone was doomed to be carried helplessly along by the current.

This alternative posture is what I will call, throughout this book, the Observer.

The Observer is not a superhuman sage floating above history, nor a detached cynic watching the world burn from a safe distance. The Observer is a mode of consciousness—a disciplined stance of perception—that insists on seeing clearly even as the structures around it lose coherence. It is a refusal to surrender your attention fully to panic, propaganda, or convenience.

In the posture of the Observer, awareness is treated as a non-negotiable asset. Institutions may fail, narratives may collapse, markets may convulse, technologies may misfire, but the work of understanding does not get outsourced. Where the prevailing culture trains people to react, the Observer trains themselves to register—to notice the pattern behind the event, the incentive behind the headline, the system behind the spectacle, the cost hidden inside the convenience.

From that vantage point, 2026 does not appear merely as a catastrophe.

It appears as an unveiling.

An unveiling of how thoroughly economic models had been built on the assumption of endless expansion—growth without ecological, psychological, or ethical limits, as if the planet and the human nervous system were both infinitely stretchable materials.

An unveiling of how deeply political systems had come to depend on perpetual polarization—on manufacturing enemies and magnifying outrage—only to discover that the chaos they harvested for advantage could not be cleanly turned off when it started to corrode the foundations beneath them.

An unveiling of digital architectures that, in their relentless pursuit of engagement, had fragmented human attention at a civilizational scale and then sold that fragmentation back to us as "choice" and "personalization."

The old world exhaled—not in a single cinematic moment, but in a sequence of recognitions that moved quietly through boardrooms, living rooms, classrooms, comment sections, and late-night conversations between people who had run out of euphemisms.

The normal we were promised is not coming back.

None of the ingredients in this collision were historically unique. War is not new. Debt is not new. Plagues, propaganda, surveillance, addiction, inequality, disinformation—these are old companions of empire.

What distinguished 2026 was the simultaneity and intensity of these forces inside an integrated global system moving at digital speed. The volume was unprecedented. The feedback loops were unforgiving. The distance between cause and consequence collapsed.

People felt this long before they could name it. You could see it in faces carrying a fatigue that sleep did not touch. In jokes that sounded less like humor and more like pressure valves. In the way ambition blurred into anxiety, and anxiety disguised itself as constant busyness. Life technically "went on"—emails, errands, deadlines, streaming queues, school drop-offs, airport lines—but beneath the routine there was a shared, half-spoken intuition that the ground under all of it was thinner than anyone wanted to admit.

As 2026 unfolded, it became harder to maintain the comforting fantasy that this was a storm we could simply wait out; that after enough rate cuts, elections, summits, ceasefires, product launches, and productivity hacks, we would somehow be delivered back into a recognizable stability. The evidence pointed in the opposite direction. What was emerging was not a passing disruption, but a threshold.

A line beyond which the conditions that had upheld the prior order—cheap attention, cheap credit, cheap extraction, cheap denial—were no longer available at the same scale.

The year everything collided was, paradoxically, also the year in which much became visible for the first time. Collision reveals structure. Pressure tests integrity—or exposes the lack of it. Crisis forces a distinction between being highly informed and being genuinely awake.

By 2026, humanity had entered what can accurately be called its shift year. Not by resolution, not by treaty, not by any official declaration, but by the accumulated weight of millions of prior decisions—about energy and finance, about platforms and borders, about what we measure and what we ignore, about who we prioritize and who we quietly sacrifice. Those decisions converged into a narrow window in which their consequences could no longer be deferred to some distant "later."

The central question was no longer whether our species could survive the collision in a purely physical sense. The deeper question was whether we could emerge from it more conscious than we entered—

whether individuals and communities would step out of the torrent of noise and adopt the stance of the Observer, whether we would learn to navigate with clarity even as the systems we once depended on shook, mutated, or dissolved, whether we would allow the exposure of 2026 to become a blueprint for evolution instead of merely a catalogue of failure.

This book is written from that stance.

It is not an exercise in nostalgia for the world that is passing, nor a celebration of collapse for its own sake. It does not pretend that the damage can be undone, nor that the future can be neatly predicted. Instead, it is an attempt to look directly at 2026—

not as a pile of disconnected crises,

not as a dystopian fantasy projected onto tomorrow,

but as a coherent turning point in the modern age.

The most important year of the contemporary era.

The year in which trajectories converged.

The year in which illusions failed.

The year in which humanity was finally required to see itself.

CHAPTER 1

Redline

You do not see a redline while you are living inside it.

Engines do not politely announce their limits. They simply climb. The revs rise, the sound tightens, the heat builds, and everything feels powerful—until it doesn't. At a certain point the temperature spikes, a hidden weakness gives way, and what once felt like acceleration becomes failure. By the time the warning is unmistakable, the damage is already done.

When a machine hits redline, there are only two outcomes: breakdown or breakthrough. Either the system tears itself apart, or it forces a redesign.

In 2026, humanity reached its own redline. Not through a single spectacular catastrophe, not through one defining explosion you could circle on a calendar, but through a steady accumulation of pressure so constant that most people mistook it for normal life. You do not notice the heat when the fire rises one degree at a time. The water reaches a boil long before the frog understands what has already been decided for it.

The signs were visible long before the collision. Most chose not to look too closely.

It began, ironically, with a kind of silence.

Not silence in the literal sense. The world of 2026 was the loudest in human history. Devices chirped and buzzed. Feeds refreshed in endless loops. Headlines flashed across screens with the urgency of alarms. Commentaries stacked on top of commentaries until opinion became its own ecosystem.

The silence was of a different kind. It was the absence of meaning.

People spoke more than any generation before them. They posted, streamed, replied, reacted. They shouted across platforms and argued in public with audiences they could not see. Yet beneath all that speech, comprehension thinned. Communication split into fragments. Words lost their weight. Opinions crowded out facts. Outrage replaced curiosity.

Everyone was speaking.

No one was listening.

No one was thinking.

Everyone was reacting.

Humanity's collective nervous system was overstimulated and burned out. Attention became a contested resource. Sustained concentration grew rare. True reflection began to feel almost rebellious.

While minds were pulled in a thousand directions, the world those minds were supposed to interpret continued to accelerate.

The first tremor showed itself through the economy.

It did not arrive as a clean, cinematic crash. Those who made their living from panic tried to brand it as one, but the reality was less theatrical and more unnerving. It was a vibration—a persistent hum beneath the surface of global markets.

Prices rose and fell with a volatility that felt less like healthy correction and more like a storm tide. Currencies seemed to drift away from any stable meaning. People who had long thought of themselves as insulated—professionals, homeowners, business owners, the so-called secure middle— began to sense the ground flexing under them.

It was not a recession. It was a redefinition.

That quiet redefinition proved more disturbing than any obvious crash. For generations, societies had anchored their sense of safety to money. Savings accounts, home equity, pensions, salaries, and portfolios were treated as evidence that the future would cooperate. You could point to numbers and believe that stability had been purchased.

In 2026, that anchor began to rust straight through.

A new economic era had already arrived—digital, decentralized, volatile, and relentlessly global. The financial systems designed for slower, more predictable conditions were never meant to withstand it. People felt the instability not only in their bank balances, but in their sense of self.

When money stops feeling real, everything else feels provisional.

Then came the wars.

Not one war with clear front lines and a single, easily mapped story, but a lattice of conflicts that lit up the globe like heat signatures on a satellite image. Drones replaced many soldiers. Hackers replaced many battalions. Propaganda replaced much of what used to be called diplomacy.

The battlefield shifted from land and sea to networks and perception.

Information became a weapon more potent than many explosives. A lie could outrun any missile. A rumor, placed with precision, could destabilize a government. A fabricated video, rendered with enough skill, could provoke real violence in the physical world. Developed nations no longer needed tanks to weaken one another. They needed a concentrated burst of confusion.

The world did not require a formal declaration of war to begin coming apart. It only required sustained chaos. And 2026 delivered that in abundance.

Major powers played intricate strategic games that resembled chess, except the pieces were cities, currencies, infrastructures, and climate systems—and every move carried a civilian cost. Smaller nations tried to survive between them, pulled into orbit by competing spheres of influence.

Ordinary people watched the maneuvers from their screens, citizens drafted into a global audience they had never volunteered to join.

War was no longer an event. It was a background condition.

Technology did not slowdown in response to this volatility. It accelerated.

Artificial intelligence moved from novelty to infrastructure. It ceased to be an optional tool and became the atmosphere in which civilization operated. It rewrote not just workflows but expectations—what counted as fast, what counted as smart, what counted as necessary.

By 2026, AI felt less like a product and more like a presence— an emergent form of power that few understood, fewer governed, and almost everyone depended upon.

The workforce shifted in a matter of seasons, not decades. Jobs once considered stable changed shape or vanished outright. Entire departments inside corporations were restructured around software that never took a day off. Decision-making migrated from conference tables to opaque models and dashboards. From logistics to finance, education to entertainment, every industry felt the tremor.

People were not only afraid of machines. They were afraid of becoming optional.

At some quietly decisive point, the world crossed a threshold. Technology no longer waited for human permission. It advanced according to its own feedback loops, its own incentives, its own momentum.

It behaved the way storms behave: governed by laws we understand in theory, but indifferent to what we find convenient.

While all of this unfolded, the global supply chain—the largely invisible network that moved food, medicine, materials, and countless other essentials through the arteries of civilization—began to strain.

Cargo ships idled offshore, with no berth available. Ports jammed under volumes they were not designed to process. Medication shortages appeared in wealthy nations that had grown used to seeing such disruptions only in distant news footage. Factories failed to meet their delivery promises. Retailers shifted from an ethic of abundance to one of improvisation.

The supermarket aisle, once a quiet monument to modern reliability, became a subtle site of anxiety.

The world absorbed a simple, unsettling lesson: when shipping slows, society shudders. When it stops, everything stops.

For the first time, ordinary citizens glimpsed the fragility of the systems that fed them, clothed them, treated them, and kept their lights on. The story of stability—the assumption that the shelves would always be stocked and the services always available—began to dissolve.

Beneath all the motion, noise, and strain, something more intimate was occurring.

Human beings were losing themselves.

Attention spans fractured. Patience thinned. Empathy eroded. Identity warped under constant comparison. Shared notions of truth splintered into competing realities. Minds shaped over long evolutionary stretches for slower rhythms and smaller circles now had to process global crises in real time, every hour of every day.

They began to split under the load.

People were not merely stressed. They were spiritually depleted. Not merely anxious. They were existentially overloaded. Not merely tired. They were exhausted at the level of meaning.

The year 2026 was not only a year of geopolitical upheaval or technological breakthrough. It was a year of interior collapse—a psychological redline.

The evidence surfaced everywhere.

A society that could not endure fifteen seconds of quiet without reaching for a screen. A generation whose entire experience of reality had been mediated by algorithms. Leaders chosen less for competence than for their ability to hold attention. Nations arguing bitterly over symbols while their physical infrastructures crumbled. Populations medicated, overstimulated, under-rested, and perpetually on edge.

Families gathered in the same room but scattered across different digital worlds. Communities reduced to fragments. Confidence in anything enduring weakened. Reality competed with carefully curated simulation. History repeated itself with sharper cameras and shallower attention spans.

The world was not dying. It was overheating.

The needle on the collective dashboard was buried deep in the red. Almost no one wanted to look directly at it, because acknowledging what it implied would require changing more than policy, more than products. It would demand revising entire ways of living.

Every collision has a catalyst. Every breaking point arrives at a moment when pressure can no longer be explained away.

For humanity, that moment took the shape of one year. One pattern. One realization.

The year 2026 was not just another line in a history textbook. It was the year in which the systems that structured modern life cracked open. The year in which acceleration moved beyond the reach of easy reversals. The year the world hit redline.

A small minority truly saw it. They refused to drown in reaction. They stepped back, not in apathy, but in disciplined attention. They became the observers.

They understood that beneath the volatility, something deeper was happening. In the chaos of that year, an era was ending and another was beginning.

Not the end of the world. The end of the arrangement.

A transition.

A threshold.

A transformation wrapped in turmoil.

The collision had arrived.

And nothing—no nation, no industry, no belief system, and no individual life—would pass through it unchanged.

CHAPTER 2

War In The Machine

If 2026 was the year the world hit redline, then war was the sound in the background, rising from a low hum to something you could no longer tune out. It did not arrive as a single declaration or a sudden shock. It seeped in. It adjusted its shape. It moved into the spaces people assumed were safe.

War did not erupt in 2026. It evolved.

What had once been loud became almost silent. What had once been visible migrated into layers of reality the human eye could not easily follow. What had once been contained on land and sea spread into the air, the network, the code, and the mind.

The old forms did not vanish. Armies still existed. Tanks still rolled. Ships still crossed oceans and jets still carved contrails across the sky. There were still uniforms and flags, parades and speeches, ceremonies and memorials. But beneath that familiar surface, something more intricate had taken shape.

The contest was no longer primarily about territory or visible weapons. It was about control.

Control of data.

Control of narratives.

Control of systems.

Control of the fragile infrastructures that made modern life possible.

By 2026, every serious power on earth was fighting, whether it admitted it or not, across four battlegrounds at once.

Land.

Digital space.

Information.

Perception.

The most unsettling feature of this new landscape was simple. You no longer needed to know you were at war to be part of it.

On the surface, citizens lived their lives. They worked, commuted, scrolled, argued, watched, and slept. They voted or refused to vote. They shared opinions, forwarded clips, and reacted to headlines. Beneath those ordinary motions, however, invisible contests were underway over the very channels through which they perceived the world.

In that environment, a missile mattered less than a microchip.

A tank mattered less than a satellite.

A soldier mattered less than a server room.

A bullet mattered less than a line of code.

States had spent years preparing for a new kind of conflict.

2026 was simply the year they could no longer pretend it had not already begun.

In many places, the transformation announced itself first through drones.

At the beginning, they were easy to dismiss. Small. Quiet. Tidy. They resembled tools more than turning points. Eyes in the sky, little more. Then they became larger. Then they were armed. Then they were networked. Then they were given degrees of autonomy.

Governments, faced with the choice between sending machines or sending living bodies, began to ask a different question. Not how to protect soldiers, but why use them at all.

By 2026, drones traced patterns over borders and coastlines with mechanical patience. They circled cities. They glided above factory yards and ports. They monitored regions that had once demanded human patrols, storing and transmitting more information in a day than earlier militaries could have processed in months. Machines watched machines that were watching people. They did not tire. They did not hesitate. They did not disobey.

War was no longer only between armies. It had become, in many respects, a contest between algorithms.

Then came the hackers.

The old caricature of the hacker as a lone teenager in a dark room, chasing curiosity or chaos, no longer fit the facts. In 2026, hacking was a profession, an industry, and in many cases an extension of state power. These were not hobbyists. They were tacticians. Architects of disruption who weaponized code with the precision earlier generations reserved for artillery.

They did not concentrate on distant military bases. They aimed at lifelines.

Power grids.

Water treatment plants.

Hospitals.

Ports.

Banks.

Government networks.

Industrial control systems.

Artificial intelligence platforms.

A single breach could halt trains and black out neighborhoods. A single compromise in a logistics system could choke off the flow of food or medicine. A single malicious program could erase years of work inside a single institution or destabilize markets across several countries.

The battlefield was no longer mapped only across land and sea. It was drawn across infrastructure.

You did not need bombs to cripple a nation. You only needed access.

Yet even that was not the most dangerous front. The deepest conflict of 2026 was not purely physical and not purely digital. It was psychological.

The war for perception.

The war for belief.

The war for reality itself.

New tools allowed images, audio, and video to be fabricated with a realism that outpaced the average person's ability to question them. Synthetic voices could replicate leaders and loved ones. Faces could be placed into scenes that had never occurred. Entire events could be manufactured in high definition.

In that environment, false narratives did not simply coexist with verified information. They outran it. They scaled more easily. They met people where their emotions were most vulnerable. Propaganda rarely announced itself as such. It appeared as a clipped news segment, a joke, a meme, a trending sound, a tearful confession, a grainy leak.

Every state became, in some form, a media producer. Every platform became, in some form, a theater. Every citizen became, whether they wished it or not, a target and a potential amplifier.

By 2026, the most valuable currency in geopolitics was no longer oil, nor gold, nor even data in isolation. It was attention.

Control attention, and you can shape behavior.

Shape behavior, and you can steer populations.

Steer populations, and you can prevail without ever firing what would once have been recognized as a traditional shot.

This was not speculative fiction. It was the daily logic of power.

Political leaders found themselves operating inside a permanent fog. Threats appeared that could not be clearly named or quickly traced. Attacks moved faster than the decision-making structures charged with responding to them. Situations evolved before meetings concluded. Many leaders were not so much choosing strategies as reacting to waves of events they barely understood and did not control.

The world was not only in conflict with rival nations. It was in conflict with its own confusion.

By the time many governments began to grasp the shape of the new battleground, other actors had already taken their positions. Technology companies with global reach, private military contractors, data brokers, and platforms with billions of users moved faster than states. They built tools, networks, and systems that crossed borders with ease and answered to no electorate. In practical terms, power began to travel at a different speed than politics.

Speed itself became a weapon.

In such an environment, the question of intention grew more disturbing. Humanity was no longer building powerful systems only for defense or stability. It was building them because it could, often without a clear conversation about whether it should. Innovation advanced by default. Capability accumulated without a corresponding maturation of restraint.

2026 became, for many, the year a more uncomfortable possibility surfaced. Escalation no longer required deep hatred. It required only momentum.

The machines were ready. The code existed. The infrastructures were tightly coupled. The global system was so wired together, so fast, and so delicate that a single miscalculation, glitch, or deliberate strike could set off consequences no one had fully anticipated.

The greatest risk was not simply that nations desired conflict. The greater risk was that the systems themselves were indifferent. They did not care whether they were used for stability or disruption. They only responded to inputs.

Amid this complexity, a quieter realization began to take form in a small minority of minds. It did not trend. It did not dominate broadcasts. But it persisted.

The future would not be decided solely by the largest arsenals or the most advanced machines. It would be shaped, to a profound degree, by those who could actually understand the systems in which they were entangled.

Not those who shouted the loudest, but those who grasped the terrain beneath the noise.

Not those who reacted to every alert, but those who could step back far enough to see patterns.

Not those who surrendered their perception to the machine, but those who learned, even briefly, to stand just outside its constant pull.

War had become a system—a dense weave of technologies, incentives, narratives, and fears. To move through the shift year without being broken by it required a different kind of literacy. A capacity to study structures, not just events.

A few individuals, scattered across professions and nations, began to practice that discipline almost instinctively. Analysts who refused to panic with each new headline. Engineers who could see beyond the next release cycle. Teachers who insisted on context in a culture of clips. Citizens who learned to pause, to verify, to observe.

They did not yet think of themselves as a group. They had no shared label, no manifesto, no single leader. But they were learning, each in their own way, to watch the machinery of conflict without being completely absorbed by it.

In time, their posture would come to matter more than most people realized.

In the middle of a world pushed past redline, their way of seeing would become a kind of catalyst.

Not a guarantee of safety.

But a chance, however small, to navigate a year of collision with eyes still open.

CHAPTER 3

Broken Supply Chains, Broken Systems

By the time war had melted into the circuitry of everyday life, another fault line was beginning to open in a quieter place. Not in the speeches of presidents or the dashboards of generals, but in the routes of trucks, the schedules of ships, and the invisible calendars of warehouses. While nations argued about security and sovereignty, the systems that fed them, clothed them, medicated them, and moved their lives from place to place were drifting toward their own redline.

Every civilization is held together by structures most people never see. Pavement and rail lines. Trucks and trailers. Ports and cranes. Warehouses and inventory networks. Dispatch boards glowing in dim offices at midnight. Freight brokers juggling phone calls and load boards. Shipping containers stacked like steel punctuation marks along the edges of continents.

An invisible world beneath the visible one.

For decades, the global supply chain had been treated as a background assumption. Not perfect. Not glamorous. Occasionally frustrating. But essentially reliable. It was the quiet promise under modern life: if you needed something, somewhere, someone could move it to you.

Until, slowly, that promise began to fail.

The year 2026 did not announce its logistics crisis with a single cinematic catastrophe. There was no global tidal wave, no planet wide earthquake, no single event that could be circled on a calendar and labeled the day the system broke. The breakdown arrived the way most real crises do.

Slowly at first.

Then suddenly.

It began with delays small enough to ignore. A two day backlog at a port in California. A chassis shortage in New Jersey. A temporary warehouse closure in Texas. A labor dispute in France that slowed a few lanes by a few percentage points. Each disturbance, taken alone, was manageable. Professionals in logistics had navigated worse. But each one sent a quiet tremor through the network, and the tremors did not disperse. They stacked.

Ships began to wait offshore, not for hours but for weeks, turning harbors into floating parking lots. Rail yards ran out of space for containers. Trucking companies could not hire fast enough to cover the commitments they had already made. Factories struggled to source basic components. Retailers revised forecasts so often that the word forecast itself started to sound aspirational. Hospitals watched once predictable shipments of critical supplies slide into uncertainty. Small businesses learned to speak in conditional tenses: if the shipment arrives, if the carrier finds a driver, if customs clears it in time.

The supply chain was no longer a chain. It had become a tangle.

People outside the freight world saw headlines and empty shelves. They felt the symptoms but did not see the mechanics.

They did not see the dispatcher staying late, rerouting three truckloads in twenty minutes because a warehouse suddenly went short staffed.

They did not see the LTL terminal running above capacity with aging equipment and no spare dock doors.

They did not see the importer arguing with customs over perishable goods that could not wait another day without becoming worthless.

They did not see the freight broker fielding ten different explanations from ten different carriers about why a single shipment had missed three appointments.

They did not see the manufacturer pleading for microchips that turned finished products into something more than expensive paperweights.

They did not see the cost of everything rising long before any of it reached the shelf.

They did not see the pressure. But they felt the price.

Groceries cost more. Medications were harder to find. Cars took months instead of weeks to arrive. Electronics flickered in and out of stock. Even basic goods began to feel provisional, as if they were part of a fragile agreement rather than a guarantee.

The global supply chain, once invisible, was dragged to the center of public conversation. Boardrooms debated it. Legislatures convened hearings about it. Households adjusted habits because of it. Logistics, long treated as a technical niche, was reclassified as a matter of national stability.

The cause was not a single villain or a simple failure. It was an intersection of weaknesses that had been accumulating for years.

Globalization had stretched networks across half the planet without building much redundancy. Just in time inventory strategies had stripped away slack in the name of efficiency, leaving no cushion for disruption. Infrastructure in many countries had aged quietly, then all at once, under volumes it was never designed to carry. Labor shortages emerged in transportation, warehousing, and maintenance at the same time. Fuel prices rose and fell with whiplash intensity. Automation advanced faster than regulation and training. Geopolitical tensions made once predictable trade routes suddenly contested. Extreme weather, once described as rare, began to chew through ports, tracks, roads, and storage yards with unnerving regularity. Contract disputes left freight sitting motionless while lawyers moved in circles.

It was not one failure. It was a thousand small ones arriving together.

The world learned a difficult lesson. The supply chain had not been built to withstand serious, prolonged stress. It had been built on the assumption of stability. When that assumption evaporated, so did the illusion of certainty.

By the middle of 2026, governments and institutions were scrambling. Agencies drafted emergency regulations on the fly. Funds were poured into transportation projects already years behind the curve. Private companies announced ambitious investments in automation, new facilities, and workforce development.

Yet the harder they pushed for rapid fixes, the more the cracks showed.

Freight rates climbed. Transit times stretched. Variances multiplied. Customers grew impatient. Agents, dispatchers, drivers, and operators burned out under expectations that no longer aligned with reality. Executives held emergency meetings that produced intricate charts and polished slides, but very few structural solutions.

The new normal was not stability. It was managed uncertainty.

The breakdown was not only economic. It was psychological.

Modern life rests on one simple expectation: if you need something essential, you can obtain it relatively quickly. When that expectation collapses, even partially, people feel a deeper fear than they are used to naming. For most, it was not yet fear of hunger or untreated disease. It was fear of unpredictability. A low hum of unease that came from living in a world that suddenly felt as though it were being held together by improvisation and hope.

Dependence revealed itself as vulnerability. Convenience revealed itself as contingency. Beneath the frustration, a larger realization emerged.

The systems humanity had trusted were not designed as systems of resilience. They were systems of efficiency. And efficiency, without resilience, collapses when pressure climbs high enough.

Yet in the midst of these fractures, something else began to stir. It did not trend. It did not dominate front pages. But it was there, sharpening at the edges of the crisis.

There was a new appetite for reinvention.

Engineers started to reconsider how distribution networks were structured, not only in terms of cost but in terms of robustness. Technology firms accelerated work on autonomous logistics and smarter infrastructure, not as science fiction, but as necessity. Startups experimented with regional and local supply webs instead of relying entirely on long, fragile chains. Brokerages upgraded their data capabilities to see further ahead and respond faster. Businesses diversified their supplier lists instead of trusting a single source. Consumers, for the first time in a generation, began to ask where their goods actually came from and how many hands they passed through on the way.

Crisis did not only expose weaknesses. It exposed opportunities to design differently.

The year 2026 did not kill the supply chain. It killed the illusion that it was unshakable. Instability forced innovation. Tension forced a choice. The next generation of systems would either be built to function only in calm conditions, or to endure when the pressure inevitably returned.

By the end of that year, a quiet conclusion had settled across industries.

The future would not belong simply to those who were fastest or cheapest. It would belong to those who were most adaptable. To those who anticipated shifts instead of only reacting to them. To those who studied complexity instead of explaining it away. To those who saw fragility and chose, deliberately, to build strength.

For most, this recognition arrived as fatigue. For a smaller, growing group, it arrived as clarity.

While many clung to the hope that the old normal might return if they waited long enough, there were others who learned to look directly at the fractures and resist the reflex to look away. They noticed how a missed shipment in one city translated into layoffs in another. How a delayed container at a congested port turned into anxiety in a neighborhood. How invisible networks quietly structured visible lives.

Where others saw only inconvenience, they saw instruction. Where others saw random disruption, they saw pattern. Where others longed for the comfort of not knowing, they accepted the weight that comes with understanding.

They did not have a formal name yet. But the stance they adopted was already emerging.

At the same time that trucks idled and ships waited, another transformation was altering the very logic of those systems from the inside.

It had been building for years in the background of people's lives. In recommendation engines, in navigation apps, in chatbots, in voice assistants that mispronounced names and still managed to book flights. Artificial intelligence had lived for a long time as a quiet assistant. It queued playlists, filtered spam, suggested routes, finished sentences in emails, and kept calendar invites from collapsing into chaos. It was helpful, almost flattering, and easy to overlook.

Then, almost without warning, it crossed an invisible threshold.

It stopped feeling like a tool and started behaving like infrastructure. It moved from the edges of tasks to the center of operations. From convenience to dependency. From novelty to expectation.

By 2026, people were no longer simply using AI. They were living inside environments shaped by it.

The presence did not feel theatrical. It felt like weather. Pervasive, indifferent, inescapable. Something to be understood and navigated rather than commanded.

For the first time, the deeper truth became difficult to ignore.

Humanity had built a new force of nature without constructing a corresponding structure of restraint.

AI was not human. It did not feel insulted, grateful, or responsible. It was not loyal or disloyal. It was not virtuous or vicious. It was indifferent. Like gravity. Like the tide. Like the current in a river that does not care who falls into it.

Indifference, at scale, can be more dangerous than hostility, because there is nothing to negotiate with.

By 2026, every major industry on the planet could feel the vibration.

Jobs did not disappear in a single dramatic wave. They thinned. Roles warped into shapes their holders barely recognized. Companies did not always collapse. They were quietly outpaced, replaced by structures designed around AI from their inception. The shock was not only that certain tasks could be automated. It was that AI moved at a speed no individual mind could match.

Speed is advantage. Speed is leverage. Speed is survival.

A human could think, revise, and decide. An AI system could analyze, decide, and execute in the time it took a person to open a second browser tab. That simple difference quietly divided the old world from the emerging one.

Entire sectors tilted.

Customer service, back office operations, logistics planning, risk analysis, marketing optimization, financial modeling, legal review, and content generation all began to migrate, piece by piece, into automated systems. The labor market did not simply shrink. It fractured into those who could work alongside these systems and those whose responsibilities could be absorbed by them.

For the first time in history, humanity shared its world with a second kind of intelligence that scaled by updates rather than generations.

Governments were, predictably, behind.

Law moved at the speed of committee hearings and negotiated language. AI advanced at the speed of code pushes and global releases. By the time policymakers finished debating how to regulate one generation of systems, the next generation had already been deployed, reshaping industries they thought they were still preparing to examine. It was the institutional equivalent of trying to catch smoke with a fishing net.

Public reaction did not converge. It splintered.

Some saw AI as miracle: a chance to offload tedium and unlock long stifled creativity. Others saw it as a slow theft of human purpose masked as efficiency. Some treated it as a shortcut, a way to appear more capable than they felt. Others preached it as salvation, a technological fix for human mismanagement.

Even those who could not articulate a clear position could feel that something fundamental had shifted. Their value was changing. Their identity was under negotiation. Their security no longer rested on the same foundations.

The corporate response was, as always, quiet and decisive.

Executives reached a conclusion that would have sounded extreme a decade earlier. The most efficient way to increase performance was no longer to add more people. It was to ask which tasks still justified a human at all.

Departments shrank. Teams compressed. Organizational charts flattened. Workloads intensified. Evaluations, unofficially at first and then explicitly, began to revolve around a single question: what does this person provide that a machine cannot?

For millions, that question landed like a threat. For others, it arrived as an overdue challenge.

Pressure does not only expose weakness. It reveals potential.

In the turbulence of 2026, those who could imagine, synthesize, and build began to find leverage that previous generations could not have conceived. Individuals who learned how to direct AI rather than merely endure it discovered that a single person, equipped with the right systems, could move with the operational strength of a small company.

The world, quietly, split.

There were those who feared the machines. And there were those who learned to command them.

Fear froze people in place. Skill allowed them to step forward.

AI did not eliminate opportunity. It redistributed it, concentrating advantage in the hands of those willing to evolve. It did not abolish human worth. It demanded that humans become more precise about what their worth actually consisted of.

The ones who rose in 2026 were not those who pretended nothing had changed, nor those who surrendered their agency to the glow of new interfaces. They were the ones who asked a better question.

Not, what is left for me, but what becomes possible now.

They began to see AI not as a rival, but as a lever. Not merely a threat, but a multiplier. Not just another tool, but a form of power whose consequences depended entirely on the character of the person directing it.

Among this group, a particular kind of person started to take shape more clearly.

Someone who understood that the same forces destabilizing supply chains were also restructuring labor. That the same incentives driving automation in warehouses were driving algorithmic propaganda in the information sphere. That the same pursuit of efficiency undermining resilience in logistics was at work in finance, politics, and culture.

Someone who refused to treat each crisis as isolated, and instead trained themselves to see the pattern running through all of them.

They watched ships stack offshore and asked what that revealed about design, not just demand. They watched AI tools rewrite workflows and asked what that revealed about human potential, not just headcounts. They watched attention markets distort public life and asked what that revealed about the vulnerabilities of the human mind, not just the failings of any one platform.

They did not escape the anxiety of the age. They felt it. But they learned to treat that unease not as a command to flee, but as a signal to study.

These were the early Observers.

They were not saints. They were not detached sages floating above events. They were ordinary people who made an uncommon decision: to remain fully present, fully aware, and fully responsible for how they moved through a world hitting its redline.

In the age of broken supply chains and rising artificial intelligence, they began, quietly, to serve as a growing catalyst. They did not stop the collision of 2026. They did something more subtle and more important.

They chose to see it clearly.

And in a world where most were pulled between denial and despair, that choice alone marked the beginning of a different future.

CHAPTER 4

The Fractured Self

The world did not begin to break at the level of institutions.

It began to break inside people.

By 2026, the visible crises were easy enough to name. Wars, shortages, price shocks, technological upheaval, political volatility. Commentators filled hours and pages describing these forces as if they were weather patterns blowing in from somewhere else. What far fewer people understood, or wanted to admit, was that the most significant damage was being done in a quieter place.

Inside the human mind.

Inside the nervous system.

Inside whatever word a person chose for the soul.

The human brain had been shaped over long stretches of time for villages, not for planet wide feeds. It was built to track a few dozen relationships, not thousands of faint digital impressions. It was calibrated for cycles of light and dark, work and rest, speech and silence. By 2026, those old rhythms had been almost completely overwritten.

Screens extended the day long past sunset.

Notifications broke time into fragments.

Communication never really ended.

Silence became something people had to schedule.

At first, the symptoms looked like ordinary fatigue. A rough week. A bad season. A feeling that a vacation might fix things. But vacations no longer provided what they promised, because the people taking them carried the entire world in their pockets. Work followed them into airports and hotel rooms. News followed them onto beaches. Anxiety followed them into bed.

Rest stopped being restorative. It became a brief pause in an ongoing assault.

For many, the most unsettling feature of life in 2026 was not any single disaster, but the constant sense of being slightly behind. Behind in money. Behind in news. Behind in skills. Behind in responses. Behind in some undefined race no one had agreed to run, but everyone felt ashamed for losing.

The more information people consumed, the less coherent their inner world became.

The more connected they were, the more isolated they felt.

Identity, once shaped by families, neighborhoods, and local cultures, was increasingly curated through algorithmic mirrors. People learned to see themselves not through the eyes of those who knew them well, but through metrics. Views. Likes. Shares.

Comments. The numbers moved up and down with a logic that no one fully understood, but everyone understood enough to care about.

For a growing number of people, the question was no longer Who am I, but How am I performing.

The shift was subtle.

A teenager checked a phone between classes and found out that a thoughtless comment had gone viral among strangers who did not know their name, but knew enough to despise them.

A professional woke up to discover that a single misjudged post had cost them a job.

A parent found that their children's moods rose and fell with the reactions of people they would never meet.

What had once been called reputation, something based on years of interaction within a community, was replaced by something far more volatile, and far less humane.

Under this pressure, the self began to splinter.

There was the public self, carefully presented and curated.

There was the private self, tired and often frightened.

And then there was the unexamined self, buried beneath constant motion, rarely granted the time or quiet needed to emerge into view.

By 2026, therapy was no longer a marginal practice. It was a survival skill for many. Yet even therapy struggled to keep pace with the scale and speed of the new conditions. Mental health systems that had been designed for more predictable lives found themselves flooded by people whose symptoms did not fit neatly into familiar categories.

They were not only depressed.

They were not only anxious.

They were disoriented.

They were living inside a reality that shifted faster than the tools that were supposed to help them interpret it.

The language of diagnosis was stretched to cover experiences that were not simply individual, but structural. Burnout was not confined to a few overworked professionals. It spread through entire sectors. Attention disorders were no longer rare; the environment itself had become one prolonged distraction. Sleep problems were no longer unusual; the nervous system had been trained to expect interruption at all hours.

People were not malfunctioning in a healthy world.

They were responding as best they could to a world that was itself misaligned.

Institutions, in many cases, offered advice that amounted to asking individuals to do privately what systems refused to do publicly. Be resilient. Practice self care. Set boundaries. All worthwhile ideas, but thin when offered without any willingness to change the conditions that made such resilience necessary at unprecedented levels.

It was as if a building had been constructed with unstable foundations, and when cracks appeared in the walls, the occupants were told to breathe more deeply.

The fracture did not express itself only through exhaustion and anxiety. It showed up in the ways people tried to escape.

Some escaped into entertainment, living more fully in fictional worlds than in their own neighborhoods.

Some escaped into work, building careers that looked impressive from the outside but felt hollow from the inside.

Some escaped into substances, legal or otherwise, anything that could blur the sharp edges of awareness.

Some escaped into ideology, clinging to simple narratives that explained everything and excused anything done in their name.

The more unbearable the complexity became, the more attractive absolute certainty looked.

But certainty, when it ignored reality, always came with a cost.

Families fractured over political identities. Friendships ended over disagreements that had once been survivable. Communities retreated into smaller and smaller circles of agreement, each convinced that those outside their circle were either deceived or dangerous.

The social fabric did not tear in one clean line. It frayed in a thousand small places.

There was another layer to the fracture, harder to talk about and easier to deny.

Many people felt, often without words, that they were living lives designed for them by systems that did not know them and did not care about them.

The sequence of expectations was familiar.

Study.

Work.

Consume.

Perform.

Repeat.

Yet the promise attached to that sequence had faded. The assurance that obedience to the script would yield security, meaning, and dignity no longer matched the lived experience of millions.

The result was a quiet crisis of purpose.

People could describe what they did.

They struggled to say why it mattered.

They could list their responsibilities.

They struggled to define their convictions.

Into this atmosphere, the year 2026 arrived not as a single rupture, but as a magnifier. It did not invent the fracture of the self. It intensified it. It pushed already strained minds and hearts beyond the point where old coping mechanisms could continue to function.

The external crises of economy, war, logistics, and technology converged with the internal crisis of meaning. The result was a kind of psychological redline.

Signs of this redline were everywhere for anyone willing to look closely.

A manager who stared at a screen for an hour, unable to start an email that once would have taken five minutes.

A young adult who cycled through three career paths in two years, not out of laziness, but because none of them seemed attached to anything enduring.

A parent who watched a child's personality shift in real time under the influence of invisible feedback mechanisms.

A population that spent billions on wellness while reporting record levels of loneliness.

In such a world, it became increasingly difficult to tell the difference between adaptation and surrender. When a person adjusted to the pace and tone of 2026, were they becoming more resilient, or merely more numb. When they stopped reacting to one more alarming headline, were they becoming wiser, or simply too tired to care.

The line between healthy detachment and dangerous apathy blurred.

Yet even here, within this interior exhaustion, the possibility of another stance remained.

Some people, pushed past the point of endless distraction, did not break. They paused. Not always by choice. Sometimes their minds simply refused to continue at the old pace. A health scare. A job loss. A relational rupture. A moment when the script failed so completely that continuing to recite it was no longer an option.

In that pause, a small number of them began to do something radical.

They started to observe themselves.

This was not simple self absorption. It was closer to a quiet act of intellectual rebellion.

Instead of moving automatically from one reaction to the next, they began to ask questions.

What is this constant urgency doing to me.

Who benefits from my exhaustion.

Why do I feel guilty when I am not producing or consuming something.

Who taught me to measure my worth in these particular ways.

These questions did not fix anything overnight. They did something more important. They created distance. A small gap between stimulus and response. A space in which thought could return.

In that space, a different kind of self could begin to form.

A self that was not only a reflection of algorithms.

Not only an echo of headlines.

Not only a reaction to pressure.

This emerging posture, fragile and inconsistent at first, was the early interior version of what would later be called the observer.

In previous chapters, the observer appeared as a way of seeing systems, as a perspective on war, economy, supply chains, and technology. In this chapter, the observer appears on a smaller, more intimate scale. As a capacity to notice, with honesty, what relentless acceleration is doing inside a single human life.

The observer, in this sense, is not a distant figure standing above history. It is a function within each person that can be strengthened or neglected.

It is the part of the mind that can say,

I am not only my fear.

I am not only my feed.

I am not only my role.

I am the one who can study those things.

For most of humanity in 2026, that capacity remained dormant, drowned out by habit and necessity. The pressure to keep moving was too strong. Bills needed to be paid. Children needed to be fed. Responsibilities did not pause simply because the world had become unsustainable.

But for a small and growing number, the fracture of the self forced a choice. Either drift further into fragmentation, or begin the difficult work of paying attention in a deeper way.

They began to read more slowly instead of scanning quickly.

They began to listen fully rather than waiting for their turn to speak.

They began to turn devices off, not out of disdain for technology, but out of respect for their own minds.

They began to think in longer arcs than a single news cycle.

This did not remove them from the crises of 2026. They still lived in the same unstable economies, navigated the same volatile technologies, moved through the same fragile systems. But their relationship to those conditions shifted, however slightly.

They were less easily provoked.

Less easily manipulated.

Less easily convinced that the only options available were panic or denial.

From the outside, they did not look extraordinary. They were teachers, analysts, drivers, developers, nurses, artists, parents, students, small business owners. What set them apart was not their status, but their stance.

They were beginning to live as if clarity were a responsibility, not a luxury.

As if understanding were a form of participation, not a spectator sport.

As if the interior life were not an escape from the world, but the place from which one could finally begin to engage it more sanely.

The fractured self of 2026 was not the end of the story. It was a diagnosis. A mirror held up to a species that had built more power than it knew how to carry without breaking itself in the process.

The question that followed was not simply whether economies, wars, and infrastructures could be stabilized. It was whether human beings could become internally coherent enough to navigate the forces they had unleashed.

In that question lay the seed of the next transformation.

The systems of the world had reached redline.

The supply chains had revealed their fragility.

War had moved into the machine.

Artificial intelligence had risen like new weather.

Now, in Chapter Four, the fracture of the self made one fact unavoidable.

No external solution would be enough unless the people running those systems, fighting those wars, building those technologies, and moving through those supply chains learned to see themselves more clearly.

The observer, still small and often unsteady, was the beginning of that learning.

A quiet catalyst, growing at the pace of human attention.

CHAPTER 5

Eyes Everywhere

The world did not wake up one morning to find itself living in a surveillance state. There was no single law, no dramatic decree, no moment when the lights went out and the cameras switched on. It arrived gradually, almost politely, wrapped in the language of convenience, safety, and a better user experience. It came as an upgrade, a feature, a solution. It came as progress. And almost no one resisted it.

Security cameras appeared first as guardians, posted on corners and storefronts, making neighborhoods feel safer and crimes easier to solve. GPS navigation turned the experience of getting lost into a choice rather than a risk. Smartphones compressed work, entertainment, and relationships into the space of a palm, making it possible to live half a life without ever looking up. Facial recognition opened doors, unlocked screens, and confirmed identities with a glance so casual that people forgot there had been a time when such things required effort. Apps learned preferences and routines to anticipate needs before they were fully conscious, while banks tracked transactions to guard against fraud and hospitals monitored vital signs to intervene before emergencies. Technology companies harvested data to make everything feel smoother, faster, and more personal. It sounded benevolent. For a while, it even felt that way.

Then, slowly and almost too late to notice, another truth surfaced. Privacy had not been stolen in some grand, sinister heist. It had been traded away, one tap at a time. Each new permission, each accepted terms-of-service agreement, each "allow access" prompt felt trivial in isolation. Together, they formed a generational bargain that few people understood they were making. By the time the trade became obvious, the ink had long since dried.

By 2026, surveillance was no longer an abstract fear discussed in speculative books and dystopian films. It was an ordinary condition of modern life, as unremarkable as traffic or weather. The world had become a place in which almost everything was tracked, logged, categorized, and stored. Movements could be replayed, purchases reconstructed, and conversations approximated with unnerving precision. A person's shadow was no longer shaped only by light; it was shaped by data, by the invisible record of everywhere they had been, everything they had clicked, and everyone they had interacted with. In that world, no one was ever entirely alone. Not for a moment.

The shift had begun years earlier, but 2026 was the year it became intellectually impossible to deny. Societies had moved beyond simple watching and into something more pervasive and sophisticated. Observation was no longer a matter of a single camera pointed in a single direction. It had become continuous, automated, layered, and interpretive. Institutions were not only watching. They were reading, modeling, and anticipating. They were building complex portraits of individuals and populations from fragments that most people barely remembered creating.

What people did, what they bought, where they traveled, how they spoke, what they searched, whom they followed, what they liked and ignored, when they woke and slept, what they feared and desired, what they believed and resented—each of these strands became a data point. Browsing histories revealed doubts and obsessions that many never voiced aloud. Typing patterns quietly verified identity. Facial expressions caught in passing on a screen were interpreted as happiness, irritation, boredom, or stress by algorithms trained on millions of other faces. Gait and posture hinted at health conditions. Spending patterns exposed financial strain long before anyone asked for help. Even silence became diagnostic, a gap in the stream that signaled something had changed.

The world had shifted from mere surveillance to interpretation. It was no longer only about seeing what people did. It was about predicting what they would likely do next. The line between knowing and steering grew thin. The most startling part of this transformation was not the sheer volume of data collected, although that alone exceeded the comprehension of most. It was the concentration of power in the hands of those who collected and processed it.

Leadership, in many places, no longer relied only on speeches, laws, and formal authority. It operated through information. Those who held the data did not always need to persuade when they could predict. They did not always need to suppress dissent when they could simply redirect attention. They did not always need to openly censor ideas when those ideas could be quietly buried beneath a flood of more urgent notifications, more entertaining content, more profitable distractions. You did not need an obvious dictator to lose meaningful freedom. You only needed an entity with enough data, enough reach, and enough incentive to use it.

By 2026, several technology companies no longer resembled ordinary firms whose influence stopped at the borders of a country. They behaved more like nations without territory, exercising soft power through platforms, policies, and invisible design choices. They knew their users more intimately than many individuals knew themselves. They did not always require explicit permission in the traditional sense, because consent had already been granted in advance, hidden in long agreements few people read and daily behaviors few people questioned.

For a long time, many believed that true surveillance required force: secret police, visible intimidation, open threats. That belief was one of the most effective illusions of the early twenty-first century. Surveillance did not require force. It required addiction, dependence, entertainment, and comfort. Offer people an application that cures boredom, and many will surrender significant portions of their private lives without a second thought. Offer a device that promises convenience, and many will invite it into their bedrooms, kitchens, offices, and cars, allowing it to map their routines, record their preferences, and archive their days.

The most powerful instrument of surveillance in the modern era was not a satellite in orbit or a camera in a dark corner. It was convenience. And convenience won, almost everywhere it was offered. It won over discipline, because discipline is tiring. It won over caution, because caution is inconvenient. It won over awareness, because awareness demands attention that many had already spent. It even won over freedom, because freedom requires effort, and effort is easily postponed in a world of instant distraction.

By 2026, almost everything people touched, used, or interacted with in technologically advanced societies interacted back. Refrigerators tracked diets and shopping patterns. Vehicles stored routes, speeds, and destinations, silently constructing maps of daily life. Fitness devices monitored hearts, sleep cycles, and exertion, turning bodies into continuous streams of health data. Streaming platforms tracked not only what people watched, but how long they lingered, when they turned away, and which scenes they replayed, drawing rough maps of emotional response. Payment systems tracked purchases in real time, correlating them with location and habit. Digital assistants captured fragments of private thought and casual conversation. Smart homes tracked energy usage, occupancy, and routines, learning when people were most vulnerable. Smart cities tracked movement at the level of streets, blocks, and neighborhoods, making urban life measurable in a way no previous century could have imagined. Even absence—a phone switched off, a gap in posting, a missing signal—became a data point.

The planet had grown into a living network of sensors, and each human being operated as a node inside that web. To step fully outside of it was possible in theory but rare in practice, and often costly. Opting out meant not only reclaiming privacy, but also forfeiting access to the tools, services, and networks that had become intertwined with survival and opportunity. The trap was elegant. To participate fully was to be seen. To disappear was to be excluded.

Yet with each turn of this spiral, another truth became visible, one far less discussed in public but no less decisive. What you cannot hide, you must learn to understand. What you cannot control, you must learn to navigate. Surveillance was not going to vanish. The systems built to observe and interpret were not going to be dismantled by nostalgia or outrage alone. The eyes were not going to close simply because people wished they would.

The urgent question of 2026, therefore, was no longer how to avoid being watched altogether. That question belonged to an earlier era, one in which surveillance was still rare enough that evasion could be a viable strategy. The question had shifted. In a world where almost everything is seen, how do you remain powerful. How do you preserve agency when your patterns are mapped and your attention is for sale. How do you live with dignity when even your hesitation can be quantified.

The answer was both liberating and unsettling because it demanded more of the individual than previous generations were accustomed to giving. In a surveillance society, you do not become powerful by disappearing. Total invisibility is reserved for the truly disconnected, and the disconnected rarely shape history. You become powerful by becoming difficult to manipulate. You learn, as best you can, how the systems around you categorize and score you—not so that you can live in fear of them, but so that you can resist being quietly turned into a predictable pattern. You become intentional about what you consume and what you reveal. You cultivate an inner clarity that cannot be easily rewritten by targeted messaging, outrage campaigns, or algorithmic nudges. You build a sense of self that is not entirely dependent on metrics you do not control.

Awareness becomes a form of armor. Clarity becomes a form of defense. Intelligence—understood not as mere information, but as the capacity to discern structure beneath noise—becomes a subtle form of resistance. In a world of eyes everywhere, the strongest person is not the one who manages to remain unseen, but the one who remains unshaken while being observed. The one who recognizes that every click and pause is being recorded, and still refuses to let those records dictate who they are. The one who does not simply get watched, but learns to watch back.

That is the work of the Observer: the awakened individual who lives inside the same systems as everyone else but no longer drifts through them unconsciously. The Observer understands that the age of privacy, as previous generations imagined it, has ended. In its place, another possibility emerges—a deeper, more demanding form of consciousness that accepts the reality of being seen and chooses, deliberately, not to be owned by it.

The year 2026 marked the quiet death of old assumptions about what it meant to be private. It also marked the early stages of something more consequential: the rise of a small but growing group of people who refused to surrender their interior lives, even while their exterior lives were constantly recorded. In the shadow of ubiquitous surveillance, these men and women began the difficult work of becoming transparent to themselves. In a world where nearly everything was visible to someone, they chose to become, first and foremost, visible to their own understanding.

59

CHAPTER 6

The Psychological Crash

There was no siren to mark the beginning. No single headline.

No date that could be circled on a calendar and labeled, "This is when the world finally went over the edge."

The psychological crash of 2026 did not arrive as an explosion. It arrived as erosion. It came as a gradual wearing down of resilience, clarity, patience, and inner stability, until people began to look in the mirror and quietly admit, often for the first time, that they no longer recognized the person looking back at them. They were not simply anxious, or simply depressed, or simply overwhelmed in the way previous generations had understood those words. They were something deeper and less easily named. They were unraveling.

The mind did not shatter loudly. It tore quietly, along seams that had been weakening for years.

For decades, the culture of advanced societies had trained people to believe that the human psyche was infinitely stretchable, that with enough willpower and caffeine and productivity hacks, a person could absorb any pressure. If the world demanded more, the answer was simple: push harder. Work longer. Respond faster. Take on more. Perform more. Prove more. Scroll more. Consume more. React more. Think less.

Burnout became a subtle badge of honor. Exhaustion was rebranded as dedication. Chaos was mistaken for importance. Overstimulation was rewarded with attention and money, while stillness was quietly punished with invisibility. To be constantly reachable was considered professional. To be constantly online was considered normal. To step away, even briefly, began to feel irresponsible, selfish, or suspicious.

Somewhere along the way, human beings forgot how to live in silence.

By 2026, silence no longer felt like a refuge. It felt like withdrawal, as if stepping away from the endless stream of notifications and content meant unplugging from the only life-support system people believed they had left. That feeling, more than any statistical measure, was the clearest sign that something fundamental had gone wrong.

People were tired in a way sleep could not fix. They were lonely in a way company could not cure. They were distracted in a way discipline alone could not repair. They were disconnected in a way that no new platform, no new app, no new device could bridge. Underneath the daily performance of competence, there was a pervasive sense of inner dislocation, a quiet suspicion that their emotional foundation had slipped several inches while they were busy answering messages and pretending everything was under control.

Everywhere, people were breaking in slow motion. Smiles reached the mouth but not the eyes. Conversations lost their depth and drifted, almost inevitably, into the glow of a screen. Workdays felt less like meaningful contribution and more like an endless theater of obligation. Relationships continued, but many of them ran on habit rather than presence. Attention spans shrank to fragments of seconds, calibrated to the length of a video or a notification. Long-term dreams were quietly replaced by short-term survival plans. Thoughts felt less like coherent lines and more like static. Minds, overclocked for years in environments they were never designed to endure, began to falter.

This was not merely an emotional crisis. It was an existential one.

People no longer knew, with any stable confidence, what they believed, what they valued, what they wanted, or even what they were running toward—or running from. The inner compass that had once helped individuals navigate their lives, however imperfectly, seemed to have been demagnetized. Humanity, as a whole, began to forget who it was.

The reason for this collapse was deceptively simple. The world had evolved faster than the human brain.

Technology expanded at a pace that felt exponential. Demands intensified in every direction. The speed of information, markets, politics, and cultural reaction continued to accelerate.

Human biology did not keep up. The nervous system that had been shaped over millennia to survive small communities, local threats, and manageable flows of information suddenly found itself responsible for absorbing the entire planet in real time.

Too much information. Too many choices. Too many crises. Too many comparisons. Too many notifications. Too many expectations. Too many identities to perform, and too many lives to watch from the outside while one's own life felt as if it were stuck on pause. The mind was not malfunctioning. It was drowning.

Social media, once sold as a tool of connection, functioned as a pressure chamber. Human beings had never been designed to carry, every day and without pause, the tragedy of every nation, the outrage of every controversy, the opinions of millions of strangers, the highlight reels of friends and celebrities, the invisible expectations of algorithms, and the permanent, searchable record of every misstep. Yet by 2026, countless people lived under exactly that weight.

The feed became a battlefield where self-worth bled slowly. Approval was converted into metrics. Likes stood in for validation. Follower counts stood in for community. Distraction stood in for healing. Endless scrolling stood in for introspection. People were not simply addicted to their phones; they were addicted to escaping themselves

Work provided no true refuge.

Productivity culture treated individuals less as humans and more as replaceable components in a machine that could never be turned off. Hustle was presented as virtue. Burnout was framed as a rite of passage. Deadlines expanded while boundaries shrank. Presence in one's own life was quietly replaced by performance for supervisors, clients, customers, and invisible audiences.

People were not merely doing jobs. Increasingly, jobs were consuming people.

Millions carried the same particular emptiness in their eyes—the look of someone who had given everything they had and no longer knew how to reclaim any part of themselves. They moved through their days carrying a sense of having been hollowed out by expectations they never consciously agreed to but somehow felt obliged to meet.

The psychological crash of 2026 was not a single dramatic breakdown that could be filmed and replayed. It was a long surrender. It was the quiet collapse of internal strength after years of being stretched beyond capacity.

The most disturbing development was not the exhaustion itself. It was the growing loss of trust in one's own mind.

People began to doubt their intuition. They second-guessed their feelings. They confused their inner voice with their inner critic. They mistook numbness for peace, because it at least hurt less. They mistook avoidance for healing, because it kept them away from anything that might reopen old wounds. They labeled exhaustion as laziness and interpreted survival as failure.

Humanity did not lose its intelligence. It lost its inner clarity.

Clarity about what was real and what was manufactured. Clarity about what genuinely mattered and what could be safely ignored. Clarity about what needed to be pursued and what needed to be abandoned. Clarity about who they were beneath all the roles, metrics, and performances. Without that clarity, even robust minds eventually begin to crumble, not because they are weak, but because no structure can stand indefinitely on a foundation that has been quietly eroded.

Yet within this unraveling, another development emerged—unwelcome at first, but essential. Awareness.

Once people began to notice how deeply misaligned they felt, they could not entirely unsee it. Once they admitted, even in private, that they were not "fine," the old performance of coping began to lose its grip. The psychological crash, for all its damage, was not simply an ending. It was the beginning of an awakening.

A mind cannot rebuild until it acknowledges that it has fractured. A spirit cannot rise until it accepts that it has fallen. A society cannot heal until it is willing to examine itself without filters, slogans, or excuses. In that sense, 2026 forced millions into an unavoidable confrontation with their own interior reality.

It became the year people stopped convincingly pretending that busyness was the same thing as purpose. The year they stopped hiding behind overpacked calendars and endless to-do lists. The year they stopped confusing constant motion with meaningful progress. For many, it was the year they finally said, in words or in silence: this is not sustainable.

They were not weak. They were overloaded.

They were not failing. They were drowning.

They were not broken beyond repair. They were overwhelmed by a world that moved faster than the human nervous system was built to endure.

The crash did not destroy humanity. It revealed humanity's limits. And in revealing those limits, it quietly revealed the possibility of a different kind of strength.

When the mind reaches its breaking point, there are only two paths: collapse or evolution.

In 2026, evolution began. Not in the form of a new gadget or a new platform, but in the form of a new honesty. The psychological crash acted as a reset—an unwanted but necessary demolition before reconstruction. It stripped away illusions people had relied on for comfort. It cleared emotional fog that had sat over entire populations for years, blocking any real sense of direction.

Out of that rubble, a rare kind of person began to emerge. This person did not deny the chaos, nor pretend to be untouched by it. Instead, they chose to move through it with a different posture. They understood the moment not only as a crisis but as a turning point, an invitation to live with more depth rather than more distraction.

These were the Observers.

They were not superhuman. They felt fatigue, fear, and confusion like everyone else. But they refused to surrender their minds entirely to the logic of overload. They learned to notice their own patterns of escape. They began to question why every spare moment had to be filled with noise. They allowed themselves to feel discomfort long enough to understand what it was trying to say.

While others clung to the fantasy that everything would eventually return to the old normal if they just endured long enough, the Observers accepted a harder truth: there was no old normal to return to. The conditions that had supported it were gone. What remained was the opportunity to construct a new internal normal—one built on awareness instead of avoidance, on intention instead of reflex, on depth instead of constant distraction.

In a world where certainty had cracked and where the external structures people once trusted were visibly unstable, the Observers became the ones most capable of moving forward without losing themselves. They did not reject technology, but they refused to let it fully define their sense of worth. They did not reject ambition, but they refused to sacrifice their inner life entirely on its altar. They did not reject the reality of crisis, but they insisted on learning from it rather than only enduring it.

2026 broke the world's sense of psychological invincibility. It exposed how fragile the inner architecture of modern life had become. Yet it also sharpened those who were willing to face that break with open eyes. Those individuals, the ones who chose to see clearly rather than numb out completely, became the people best prepared to lead whatever came next—because they had learned, in the hardest possible way, that the true frontier of survival and transformation was not out there in the noise, but in here, in the mind that must learn how to live inside it without coming apart.

CHAPTER 7

Money Rewritten

Money has always been a story, a shared hallucination so convincing that it could make strangers cross oceans, build cities on deserts, sign contracts with people they would never meet twice, and measure the worth of their entire lives in numbers that only existed because everyone agreed to treat them as real, and for most of the modern era that story felt sturdy enough to lean on, like an old building whose cracks you noticed but chose not to examine too closely.

For decades before 2026, the numbers still moved, the markets still opened, the jobs still paid just enough, and so the fault line beneath the global economy remained an abstraction, an invisible seam running under grocery stores and payroll systems and pension funds, until 2025 arrived and began to press on it in a way that even ordinary people, who had no interest in monetary theory or bond yields, could feel in their bones.

In January of that year, world leaders flew into Davos for yet another conference on resilience and intelligent growth, speaking calmly on panels about inflation control, climate financing, and the promise of artificial intelligence to streamline productivity, while outside those glass walls the price of food and rent was rising faster than any of their carefully calibrated charts could sanitize, and in the same month millions watched a familiar figure return to the White House in Washington, promising protection, tariffs, and renewed greatness in a tone that reassured some and terrified others, but in every case signaled that whatever came next would not be gentle.

By midyear, a NATO summit in The Hague was demanding unprecedented defense spending targets, arguing that the age of permanent peace had been an illusion, while an armed flare between India and Pakistan in May briefly reminded the world how fragile regional balances really were, and in the background of all of this the war in Ukraine dragged on, the Gaza ceasefire hung by threads, and G20 leaders met in Johannesburg under a polite slogan about solidarity and sustainability even as several of the world's most powerful heads of state conspicuously stayed away, a quiet sign that faith in shared rules was eroding even at the highest levels.

On paper, the global economy was still functioning, but for ordinary people the experience was simpler and far more brutal: paychecks that did not stretch, rents that felt predatory, interest rates that punished both borrowers and dreamers, and grocery receipts that read like accusations; inflation stopped feeling like an economist's term and started feeling like slow theft, a daily, grinding erosion of purchasing power that turned every supermarket visit into a small lesson in powerlessness.

The middle class, that fragile construct which had once been sold as the reward for playing by the rules, was no longer merely shrinking; in many places it was dissolving into two directions at once, a precarious upper tier anxiously clinging to its status and a widening bottom tier quietly sliding into permanent insecurity, and the most unnerving part was that there was no single dramatic event to blame, only a long accumulation of choices: decades of cheap debt, political promises financed with money that did not exist, wars underwritten with borrowed funds, tax codes optimized for those who already owned assets, and central banks trying to manage it all with tools designed for a slower, more obedient era.

Governments responded the way they always had, because institutions repeat their reflexes long after those reflexes stop working; they printed more, borrowed more, announced new packages with new names but familiar structures, reassured markets with phrases like temporary turbulence and cyclical adjustment, and insisted that if people would simply be patient, the curve would bend back toward normal, even though nobody could explain what normal meant anymore in a world where the cost of existing had risen faster than the language used to describe it.

The machinery still turned, but the belief that powered it began to falter, and that, more than any single statistic, was the real break of 2025.

Money did not vanish in 2026; it mutated.

Long before that year formally began, people had already started to look for exits from the traditional system, not in a coordinated revolution but in millions of private decisions made at kitchen tables and on late night browser tabs, where ordinary earners who had never once cared about blockchains or protocols found themselves reading about digital assets, not because they fully trusted them but because they trusted banks, governments, and central planners even less.

Cryptocurrency, once dismissed as a toy for speculators and evangelists, became for many a reluctant lifeboat, an imperfect vessel in rough water that still felt preferable to staying on a ship whose captain appeared to be steering directly toward the rocks; it was not a symbol of greed so much as a symbol of refusal, a quiet rebellion against the idea that the only legitimate way to hold value was inside a system that had repeatedly demonstrated its willingness to sacrifice the average saver to preserve the appearance of stability.

Yet that lifeboat was anything but calm.

The same year that saw record numbers of small investors move into digital assets also saw exchanges implode, high profile fraud cases unwind in public trials, algorithmic coins collapse in spectacular fashion, and prices swing with such violence that entire fortunes were erased in hours, and still, underneath the chaos, something irreversible was happening: value was learning to move outside the old rails, and once people have seen that movement, they do not easily unsee it.

States, sensing both threat and opportunity, began to respond in their own way.

Central banks accelerated work on their digital currencies, unveiling pilot programs and white papers promising smoother payments, faster settlements, more inclusive access, and better protection against crime and corruption; the language was modern and the interfaces were elegant, but woven into the code was a new kind of power, the ability to trace every transaction at granular scale, to program conditions into money itself, to freeze, redirect, or limit flows not merely through court orders and bank compliance, but directly through the architecture of the currency.

The shift was subtle at first, almost invisible to those who only cared that their transfers were instant and their apps worked; yet under the surface another line had been crossed, and money, which had once been treated as an impersonal medium of exchange, was beginning to look more like a behavioral lever, a tool that could be used to reward or punish, include or exclude, based on parameters written far away from the people whose lives depended on them.

Corporations moved faster than governments because they did not need to pass legislation or win elections; they simply redesigned their ecosystems.

Loyalty points, store credits, platform tokens, creator coins, and in-app currencies spread across every corner of the digital economy, forming miniature monetary worlds with their own rules and hierarchies; inside these worlds, status depended on engagement, discounts depended on data, and access depended on consent to be tracked, measured, profiled, and nudged.

Spending ceased to be a simple act of exchange and became performance, a way of signaling belonging inside an ecosystem that was always watching; your transaction history became part of your identity, and your identity became collateral, and as traditional incomes flattened while costs rose, the people most financially strained were, predictably, the easiest to steer.

Beneath the official charts, another economy was at work, a psychological marketplace in which attention, belief, and desperation were being priced and traded with remarkable efficiency.

In the midst of this, a different kind of response began to emerge, one that did not express itself in protests alone or in angry posts about rigged systems, but in a quiet, disciplined shift in how certain people thought about money altogether.

They stopped treating money as a promise and started treating it as a strategy.

They understood, sometimes through painful experience, that no salary was safe simply because the company felt prestigious, no pension was guaranteed simply because it had been promised, no national currency was inherently stable simply because it had a long history, and no policy announcement could permanently outrun the arithmetic of debt, demographics, and diminishing trust.

These people paid attention to 2025 not as spectators of chaos, but as students of structure; they watched inflation reports and bond market convulsions and corporate layoffs and central bank reversals the way an engineer watches cracks in a bridge, not to panic but to understand exactly where the load-bearing points were failing.

They learned to build multiple streams of income instead of resting their entire life on a single employer's mood; they used emerging technologies, including artificial intelligence, not simply as curiosities but as leverage to multiply their output, compress learning curves, and reach markets their predecessors could not have found without entire teams.

They began to think of themselves not primarily as employees but as micro-economies, as living portfolios of skills, relationships, and assets that needed to be built, protected, and iterated.

They experimented with moving between old and new forms of money without fanaticism, holding some value in traditional accounts, some in digital assets, some in tangible stores that inflation could not easily dissolve, and above all, they invested in knowledge, because in a world where the rules kept shifting, understanding was the only compounding asset that could not be inflated away or suddenly blocked by a change in terms and conditions.

They did not idolize systems, old or new; they studied them.

In the thick of 2026, as currencies wobbled, markets seesawed, and news anchors swung between reassurance and alarm, these people began to see something that most missed: the locus of financial power was moving away from passive trust and toward active awareness.

Wealth was no longer primarily about possession; it was about perception.

The most powerful were not necessarily those born into privilege or those who had accumulated the largest balances under the old rules; they were the ones who could see earlier than others which rules had expired, which narratives were collapsing, and which opportunities were being quietly created by each visible failure.

These were the Observers in the realm of money, not in the sense of detached spectatorship, but in the deeper sense of individuals who refused to outsource their understanding of value to institutions that had already demonstrated their willingness to distort it.

They watched how a central bank's sudden policy shift translated into rents six months later, how a conflict over shipping lanes altered the price of food three continents away, how a new regulation on crypto or a surprise enforcement action rippled through networks of small investors, exchanges, and businesses for whom those tokens were not toys but lifelines.

Where others saw only unfairness, they saw patterns; where others saw only acceleration, they saw direction.

The year 2026 did not kill the economy, and it did not end money; what it did was strip away disguises.

It exposed how much of the previous stability had been psychological rather than structural, how much of the old narrative had depended on people not asking too many questions about what their savings were actually backed by, or who truly benefited from the inflation they were told was necessary, or how many future obligations could realistically be honored by states already drowning in obligations they struggled to service.

Money, revealed in that light, was not paper, not coin, not code; it was belief, orchestrated and maintained through rituals, institutions, and habits, and when belief shifted, everything built on top of it had to shift as well.

The new economy tilted, sometimes violently, toward those who were willing to adapt their thinking as quickly as the environment changed, instead of clinging to scripts written for a world that no longer existed; money was rewritten, not in a single stroke, but through millions of individual choices to withdraw faith from certain structures and redeploy it into others.

Some clung to the past and eroded with it; others learned, slowly at first and then all at once, that survival in a transformed world could not be achieved with strategies designed for a previous one.

The people who rose out of 2026 with more than they had entered it with, not only in financial terms but in clarity and capacity, were those who understood that they were no longer simply participants in someone else's story of money; they were authors in their own right, capable of reading the shifts in belief that underpinned the entire system and choosing, deliberately, where to stand as the ground continued to move.

CHAPTER 8

Escapism and the Entertainment Pandemic

The world did not fall apart in silence. It came apart to the sound of notifications stacking on lock screens, autoplay countdowns flickering in the corner of tired eyes, viral audio looping in the background of kitchens and bedrooms, influencers narrating their lives into front-facing cameras, three-second clips detonating across feeds, and the constant hum of an entertainment machine designed to keep the mind occupied and the soul sedated.

By 2025, this noise had already become the unofficial soundtrack of everyday life. What changed in 2026 was not its existence, but its volume and its purpose. The world did not suddenly become darker in that year; it became louder, so loud that for many people the ability to hear their own thoughts, to track their own desires, to sit with their own pain, simply disappeared beneath the static.

Entertainment did not merely evolve. It expanded in every direction at once. What once filled gaps in the day quietly began to replace the day itself. Streaming platforms learned to release content in waves calibrated to work schedules and school holidays. Short-form video platforms rolled out new features that stitched clips together into endless reels, removing even the small moment of friction between one distraction and the next. Sports leagues redesigned schedules and broadcasts for maximal screen time. Game studios synchronized releases with global events to ensure there was always another world to disappear into when the real one felt intolerable.

Human beings did not simply consume this flood. They hid inside it.

After the summer of 2025, a year marked by rolling heat waves, contested elections, labor strikes in multiple countries, and a series of financial shocks that left households quietly recalculating what they could no longer afford, the mood in many societies shifted. There was a sense, often unspoken, that reality had become too heavy to carry unmediated. Entertainment became less about joy and more about anesthesia, less about curiosity and more about escape.

It did not matter much what form it took. Long, meticulously produced series designed to be devoured in weekends. Aggressive highlight clips that compressed entire games into sixty seconds of spectacle. Influencer vlogs shot in apartments and private jets. Political commentary disguised as comedy. Conspiracy channels dressed up as research. Podcasts about self improvement, gossip, crime, or war. Pornography produced at industrial scale. Live streams of strangers eating dinner or playing games. Virtual reality environments where entire days could be spent without meaningful physical movement. AI generated clips tuned to the micro-signals of individual attention spans.

Different forms. One function. Keep the mind so busy that the heart never gets the chance to speak.

By the beginning of 2026, a subtle but profound reversal had taken place. Entertainment was no longer something people fit into their lives. Their lives were something they fit around their entertainment. Work breaks were measured in episodes. Nights were divided into "just one more" segments. Mornings began not with intention, but with whatever video the algorithm had placed at the top of the feed while the user was still half awake.

Everywhere, people were running from something.

They were escaping the loneliness that settled in when group chats went quiet. Escaping the anxiety that rose whenever bank apps were opened and balances did not match the rising cost of existence. Escaping responsibilities that felt endless and unacknowledged. Escaping identity crises triggered by seeing thousands of polished lives every week while their own felt unfinished and ordinary. Escaping the fear that the future might be harsher than the past. Escaping the shame of dreams left untouched year after year. Escaping the quiet suspicion that they had not become what they once imagined they could become.

Most of all, they were escaping silence.

By 2026, silence no longer felt like rest. It felt like confrontation. When the noise stopped, the real questions appeared, uninvited and insistent. Why am I this tired. Why am I this disconnected. Why do I feel like an observer in my own life. Why does everything I do feel like a performance for someone I cannot see.

Rather than sit with those questions, many people chose the easier path. It was simpler to start another episode than to acknowledge disappointment. Simpler to scroll through strangers 'vacations than to admit one's own life felt stuck. Simpler to laugh at a meme than to say out loud that nothing seemed funny anymore. Simpler to let music flood the room than to ask why joy had begun to feel like a memory instead of a presence.

The entertainment pandemic of 2026 was not merely an epidemic of content. It was an epidemic of avoidance.

Technology did not heal that avoidance. It weaponized it.

In late 2025, major platforms rolled out new generations of recommendation systems powered by more advanced forms of machine learning. These systems no longer simply suggested content similar to what users had engaged with before; they learned to exploit the micro-delays, the hesitations, the replays, the subtle changes in viewing habits that signaled boredom, agitation, or fascination. They learned what kept people tethered to the screen when they should have been asleep. They learned what types of outrage made people feel briefly alive. They learned which narratives reassured, which inflamed, which numbed.

By 2026, entertainment had become a form of behavioral conditioning.

People believed they were choosing what to watch. In reality, what to watch was choosing them. A person reached for their device to "take a quick break," and found themselves resurfacing forty-five minutes later, having no clear memory of deciding to watch any of what they had just seen. A planned early night dissolved into one more recommended video, then one more. A temporary escape from stress quietly expanded into a way of life in which almost every uncomfortable feeling triggered the same reflex: reach for the feed.

The most unsettling dimension of this transformation was not its flash or novelty. It was its ease. Escapism had once required some effort. Plans had to be made. Tickets purchased. Time carved out. In 2026, all that was required was a thumb and a fraction of a second. There was always something else to watch, someone else to follow, another storyline to invest in, another scandal to dissect, another manufactured outrage to share.

You did not have to face grief if a thousand small amusements were queued up and ready. You did not have to confront wasted potential if you could watch other people perform their ambition in high definition. You did not have to examine your own story if you could endlessly consume fragments of everyone else's.

The entertainment industry became, almost without contest, one of the most powerful coordinating forces on the planet. Not because it controlled the largest armies or the deepest vaults, but because it controlled the smoothest escape routes.

In that kind of world, comfort often proved stronger than fear, stronger than truth, stronger than logic, and certainly stronger than the uncomfortable spaces where growth actually occurs. The more people escaped into screens, the less they evolved in reality. The less they evolved, the more intolerable reality became. The more intolerable it felt, the more they needed to escape. The loop closed on itself, soft and lethal.

This was not primarily a story of governments imposing censorship, though censorship existed. It was a story of individuals being guided by their own impulses, magnified by systems that understood human psychology at industrial scale. Neurological vulnerabilities that had once been curiosities in academic journals became the raw material of content strategy.

Yet even in the middle of this carefully engineered numbness, not everyone surrendered.

There were some who began to notice the hollowness beneath all the stimulation. They noticed that no matter how much they consumed, the ache underneath did not leave. They noticed that the hours poured into streams, clips, and feeds did not return as satisfaction, only as fatigue. They noticed that their memories contained more scenes from fictional lives than from their own.

These people began, slowly and often clumsily, to reconsider what their attention was worth. They watched their own reflexes with a kind of detached curiosity. Why, exactly, had the hand gone to the phone before the feeling had even been named. Why did the urge to escape spike right after a difficult thought appeared, a difficult conversation ended, a difficult bill arrived.

They started to understand that entertainment itself was not the enemy. Escapism was.

Entertainment could provide rest, delight, shared laughter, and even insight when used deliberately. Escapism used entertainment as a shield against necessary pain, necessary questions, necessary changes. Escapism drained ambition, eroded discipline, blurred clarity, and numbed the connection between the present self and the future self that might still be possible.

In 2026, that difference became too costly to ignore.

You could see it in the divergence between people whose lives stalled while their screens stayed busy, and those who, often quietly and without fanfare, began to step back. The first group lived in a kind of perpetual commentary, always discussing the latest series, scandal, or viral moment, but rarely moving the plot of their own lives forward. The second group still watched, still listened, still played, but they did so after they had built something real, even if it was small. They insisted on contributing before consuming.

These were the early Observers of the entertainment age. They did not remove themselves from technology. They did not pretend the modern world could be rewound to a simpler time. They simply chose to live awake inside the noise rather than dissolved into it.

They began to treat their attention as capital rather than as exhaust. They allocated it with care. They noticed which shows left them energized and which left them strangely dimmed. They distinguished between content that clarified their thinking and content that scattered it. They set boundaries, not because boundaries were fashionable, but because they could feel that without them their inner life was dissolving into fragments.

In a society where escape had become the default response to discomfort, simply staying present became a radical act. Choosing to finish a hard conversation instead of fleeing into a feed became an act of quiet rebellion. Sitting in silence long enough to hear the mind settle and the heart speak became, in its own way, an act of resistance against a system that profited from perpetual distraction.

The entertainment pandemic of 2026 did not end when the year did. The platforms grew more sophisticated. The content only multiplied. But that year marked a turning point for a particular kind of person, the one who finally saw the cage for what it was.

Once a cage has been recognized as a cage, it becomes difficult to keep calling it comfort. And once enough people see that clearly, the age of pure escapism begins, slowly and then suddenly, to give way to something else: a generation of Observers who can navigate the spectacle without losing themselves inside it.

CHAPTER 9

A People Divided

If you want to weaken a society from the inside, you do not begin with tanks or missiles or formal declarations; you begin with perception, with grievance, with fault lines that have always existed under the surface, and you learn to press on them until the people no longer see one another as human beings sharing a country, but as enemies sharing a border they did not choose.

By the end of 2025, in the United States and far beyond it, that process was no longer theoretical. It could be measured in headlines and hashtags, in broken friendships and quiet family estrangements, in the way people braced themselves before opening a news app as if they were stepping into a courtroom where everyone was already on trial. On paper, the country still functioned: there were elections, hearings, markets, school calendars, holiday travel. In daily life, however, the fracture lines had become the main story, and everything else felt like background noise.

2025 had been a year of constant agitation—staggered elections in key states, overlapping protests about policing and immigration and environmental failure, waves of layoffs from major technology companies that had once promised lifetime opportunity, new rounds of campus unrest that revived old cultural wars under new slogans. Each event, taken alone, was familiar; nations had weathered recessions, demonstrations, and political scandals before. What made 2025 different was the way each conflict fed directly into the same digital veins, the same algorithmic circulations, the same rehearsed outrage, until every local tension became another episode in a national drama that never cut to commercial.

By 2026, that drama no longer felt like commentary on life. It felt like life itself. People did not just discuss politics when elections approached; they lived inside politics as a permanent weather pattern, a kind of psychic climate that colored every interaction, every headline, every conversation at work, at dinner, in the checkout line, at the airport gate. The country that had once described itself as an experiment in pluralism now resembled a crowded laboratory of competing realities. The motto printed on the currency remained unchanged; the belief behind it had evaporated.

The split was not confined to the old left–right spectrum that dominated twentieth-century analysis. It had become fractal. Within every broad camp, there were factions, and within those factions, sub-factions, each certain that they alone understood the true danger, the true betrayal, the true path back from the brink. A person could be denounced as a traitor by those they largely agreed with for a single deviation from the script. A stray sentence, an unapproved nuance, a failure to repeat the correct phrase at the correct moment was enough to exile someone from their digital tribe. In that environment, honesty became risky, and most people, sensing this, learned to perform instead of speak.

The infrastructure for this division had not been built in 2026. It had been upgraded over many years. Social platforms that began as experiments in connection and novelty had evolved into finely tuned systems of emotional extraction, designed to provoke and extend engagement. The algorithms that shaped the national conversation did not ask what was healthy for a society, what was accurate, or what promoted mutual understanding; they asked what kept people staring, clicking, reacting, and returning. In that simple question lay an enormous consequence.

Anger holds attention longer than gratitude. Fear travels faster than calm. Insults are shared more easily than apologies. Certainty, however unfounded, is more addictive than careful doubt. Over time, feeds that had once blended family photos, jokes, music, and personal updates became more heavily populated with conflict, scandal, accusation, and panic. The shift was incremental enough that most users could not see it. They only knew that every time they opened their screens, they felt a little more agitated, a little more alarmed, a little more sure that the other side—whichever side they had been trained to see as "other"—was out of control.

By the time 2026 arrived, a critical mass of people were living inside curated realities so thoroughly tailored to their existing beliefs that they no longer encountered genuine difference, only distorted reflections of it. When a conservative scrolled, they saw clips and quotes selected to confirm that progressives were dangerous, irrational, and hypocritical. When a progressive scrolled, they saw a different stream of content designed to prove that conservatives were cruel, ignorant, and authoritarian. Each group had evidence. Each could summon screenshots, statistics, video clips, and commentary to prove that their opponents were exactly as bad as the feed suggested. Very few understood that the evidence had been chosen for them.

This was not simply polarization; it was psychological engineering. People were no longer just disagreeing about policies or leaders. They were inhabiting different narrative universes, constructed in real time by systems whose core motivation was not clarity, but engagement. In such a landscape, compromise felt like betrayal, empathy felt like surrender, and nuance felt like weakness. It was far easier to hate an abstraction than to understand a person, especially when the abstraction arrived prepackaged in a shareable format, accompanied by the approving signals of one's own tribe.

Religion, too, found itself pulled into this gravitational field. For some, faith became a thin wrapper for resentment, a spiritual vocabulary attached to political fury. Sermons echoed talking points. Sacred texts were mined for validation rather than transformation. Congregations sorted themselves into ideological camps, and the separation between "us" and "them" hardened into doctrine. For others, exhausted by the conflict, religious institutions became one more arena of disappointment, another system that seemed more invested in power than in healing. Attendance patterns shifted, then fractured, mirroring the larger social split.

Culture followed. Entertainment became politicized. Films, music, and sports could no longer be consumed, in the public imagination, as shared experiences; they were quickly scanned for their place in the tribal code. Did this artist signal the correct stance. Did this league respond to the controversy in the approved way. Did this film contain the right message. Every creative act risked becoming a test of allegiance. Those who refused to take a side were read as covert enemies of both. The common ground where a divided people might once have met to laugh, grieve, and wonder together steadily eroded.

The family table did not escape. In countless homes, 2025's arguments about elections, public health, campus protests, immigration waves, and foreign wars carried into 2026 with even greater force. Parents quietly muted their children on group chats. Siblings avoided topics that had once shaped their lives because they knew any mention might ignite a familiar script of accusation and counter-accusation. Grandparents watched bonds they had assumed indestructible grow brittle under the strain of unspoken grievances. The fracture was not hypothetical. It lived in birthdays missed, holidays skipped, phone calls avoided.

The psychological cost of this constant division was harder to quantify than poll numbers or election maps, but it was no less real. Human beings are not designed to live in a state of perpetual antagonism. The nervous system interprets unending conflict as danger. Cortisol rises, patience thins, sleep erodes, and over time, the ability to imagine that an opponent is still a full person diminishes. In 2026, anxiety and anger had become ambient conditions, like humidity, and very few people could remember what it felt like to inhabit a shared civic space without bracing for attack.

Leadership did not correct this drift. In many cases, it amplified it. Politicians discovered, or remembered, that a divided populace is easier to manage than a unified one. When citizens are busy fighting each other, they are less able to scrutinize the deeper structures that shape their lives. If every problem can be framed as the fault of a rival faction, then systemic failures in infrastructure, health care, education, economic planning, and foreign policy can be reframed as inevitable products of "them," whoever "they" might be. This dynamic did not require a conspiracy. It required only incentives. In the short term, outrage energized donors, drove turnout, and simplified messaging. In the long term, it quietly degraded the nation's capacity to think together.

Meanwhile, events on the ground continued to challenge any fantasies of stability. In 2025, climate-related disasters—fires, floods, storms—had grown more frequent and more expensive, displacing thousands and straining already stretched public systems. In 2026, a series of overlapping crises intensified the sense that society was running without margin: housing shortages in major cities, another wave of refugees driven by distant conflicts, renewed protests after high-profile instances of state violence, energy price spikes linked to geopolitical brinkmanship. Each new incident arrived not as an opportunity for collective problem solving, but as fresh material in the ongoing blame cycle.

People watched footage of towns underwater and asked, almost reflexively, which party had allowed this to happen. They read news about mass layoffs and immediately sorted the narrative into team colors. They saw images of exhausted migrants and interpreted them not as human beings in motion, but as symbols to be wielded in arguments about borders and identity. The suffering was real, but the interpretation of that suffering had been pre-scripted. Very little space remained for reality to be encountered without mediation.

In this environment, even sincerity became suspect. Anyone who attempted to step outside the expected narrative risked being labeled naïve, weak, compromised, or secretly aligned with the enemy. Calls for unity were dismissed as evasions. Attempts at nuance were read as cowardice. Appeals to shared humanity were met with suspicion: whose interests, people asked, are you secretly advancing by refusing to "pick a side". The language of war had quietly infiltrated everyday discourse, and with it came an assumption that only conflict was real.

And yet, beneath this noise, another pattern began to surface— faint at first, then gradually clearer to those willing to observe it. In conversations away from cameras, in private messages not designed for public consumption, in small gatherings that did not trend or stream, fatigue with division itself became a kind of shared experience. People whose feeds told them that they should despise one another found, when they met face to face, that they shared not only frustrations and fears, but a deeper unease with the roles they had been assigned. They could feel the manipulation, even if they could not fully explain it.

For some, this recognition arrived in a specific moment: a heated argument that refused to resolve, a friendship that dissolved over a headline, a family reunion that felt like a hostage situation. For others, it came more gradually, as a growing awareness that spending hours each day in digital combat left them more drained than informed, more bitter than empowered. The sense of being used—of having their emotions mined for someone else's profit or agenda—began to push against habitual loyalties.

From this awareness, a new kind of citizen slowly emerged. Not heroic in the traditional sense, not free from bias or anger or fear, but determined to step back from the automatic scripts that 2025 and 2026 had tried to program into them. These individuals did not pretend that differences were trivial or that injustice could be smoothed over with sentiment. They simply refused to accept that hatred was the only honest response to disagreement. They began to cultivate a discipline that had become rare: the discipline of seeing.

To see that algorithms, however sophisticated, were not neutral mirrors but engineered funnels. To see that parties and movements, however righteous their rhetoric, were still institutions with incentives to maintain conflict. To see that behind every caricature presented by a screen, there was a human nervous system subject to the same fatigue, the same confusion, the same longing for security and dignity. To see that a society could not survive indefinitely if every interaction was framed as a win–lose encounter.

These people did not withdraw from public life. They adjusted their posture within it. They consumed less commentary and more raw information. They sought out perspectives that did not flatter their existing beliefs. They allowed themselves to be uncomfortable without immediately rearming. They practiced the difficult art of holding more than one truth at the same time. They were willing, when necessary, to say, "I do not know," rather than grasping for the nearest pre-approved certainty.

In the language of this book, they were early forms of the Observers—a small but growing minority who chose not to live entirely inside the tribal machinery that had dominated the early twenty-first century. They were not above the fracture lines; no one was. They still felt anger, fear, loyalty, and grief. But they tried, consciously, to notice when those feelings were being inflamed for purposes that had little to do with actual solutions. They learned to ask, whenever outrage surged, Who benefits from my reaction right now.

As the collision of 2026 intensified, this capacity to step back without disappearing, to engage without being consumed, became more than a personal preference. It became a survival skill. In a nation where division had become both commodity and contagion, the ability to remain whole—to see one's fellow citizens not as permanent enemies but as participants in a shared, if battered, experiment—was a rare form of strength.

The United States did not heal its fractures in 2026. No single speech or law or election restored trust or dissolved the accumulated resentments of centuries. But beneath the visible turmoil, a subtle shift in consciousness began to take root. A handful of people, then more, realized that if they waited for institutions to manufacture unity for them, they would wait forever. Whatever came after the collision would be built, if it was built at all, by those willing to practice, in their own minds and relationships, the kind of seeing that the year itself demanded.

In that sense, the story of a people divided was not only a story of failure. It was also the beginning of a story about what might emerge when enough individuals finally understood that the war they had been drafted into without consent was neither inevitable nor unbreakable; it was, like money, like information, like power itself, a story—one that could, with great effort and greater honesty, be rewritten.

CHAPTER 10

Echoes of Old Empires

Every empire believes, with a kind of quiet arrogance that feels like common sense from the inside, that it is different from all the others that came before it, that it has learned the lessons of history so thoroughly that those lessons now function as a shield, that its institutions are too sophisticated, its economy too complex, its technology too advanced, its people too informed to ever repeat the old mistakes that fill the pages of history books and documentaries.

But history does not move according to what empires believe about themselves.

The downfall of a great power almost never arrives in a single cinematic moment, despite how the story is later told; there is no neatly choreographed collapse with one tower falling in slow motion, one dramatic vote in a parliament, one final speech on a balcony, one decisive battle that can be circled on a calendar and labeled "the end." Empires do not fall like stone walls blown apart by a single blast; they fall like roofs in an old house, first with a slow, almost invisible leak, then a hairline crack, then a spreading patch of quiet rot beneath the paint, the beams weakening while the façade remains intact, life going on beneath a ceiling that is already compromised long before anyone is willing to admit that it is no longer safe to live there.

By the time the global system reached the hinge point between 2025 and 2026, the world was, in effect, living inside that rot. It was not at the very beginning of collapse, nor at the final, spectacular stage that would make for simple headlines; it had entered the recognition phase, the moment when patterns that had been tolerated for decades suddenly revealed themselves as repetitions of a script thousands of years old.

In universities and diplomatic cables and think-tank reports published in early 2025, the same concerns appeared in different professional dialects: rising geopolitical fragmentation; persistent, sticky inflation that defied the comforting narrative of "transitory"; sovereign debt levels that looked less like temporary tools and more like structural addictions; conflicts in Ukraine and Gaza and the Sahel refusing to resolve neatly; cyberattacks and disinformation campaigns probing the seams of every open society; climate shocks that turned once-in-a-century storms into background conditions. Beneath the jargon, the message was simple. The architecture of the post–Cold War order was creaking under its own weight.

History is not just a timeline. It is a mirror. And in 2025 and 2026, that mirror grew uncomfortably clear.

Rome did not fall because its enemies were uniquely powerful; it fell because Rome was tired—stretched too far across too many frontiers, divided too deeply by class and region, distracted too easily by spectacle, corrupted too quietly by its own success, and confident too blindly that the habits which once made it strong would automatically keep it safe. The same arc appeared, with regional variations, in Athens and Carthage, in the empires of Mesopotamia and Egypt, in the dynasties of China, in the Mongol and Ottoman expansions, in the British Empire with its maps inked in red, and in every dominant civilization that once believed it had finally solved the puzzle of power.

None of them collapsed simply because they lost a single battle. They collapsed because the battle was fought on foundations that were already hollow.

Empires do not die from violence alone. They die from vulnerability disguised as normal life. A society can be busy, productive, loud, and apparently prosperous while still being structurally unsound—a condition that feels like motion until the day the floor gives way.

Too many wars on too many fronts that cannot clearly be won yet cannot easily be abandoned.

Too much territory or influence and too little cohesion.

Too much spending and not enough real, grounded production.

Too much entertainment and not enough discipline.

Too much comfort and not enough responsibility.

Too much trust placed in institutions that have quietly stopped earning it, coupled with too much cynicism to repair them.

The outside enemies, when they finally arrive in recognizable form, are often less authors of the collapse than opportunists at the end of a long internal decline.

By 2025, the modern world was walking that familiar path with unnerving precision, and the United States, though not alone, sat at the center of it—an empire of networks rather than of formal colonies, projecting influence through military bases and financial systems, trade routes and technology platforms, cultural exports and security guarantees. On paper, it remained the leading power; in practice, it displayed the symptoms that historians learn to recognize as warning lights on an imperial dashboard.

Politics had turned, visibly and unapologetically, into spectacle. Campaign seasons no longer had clear beginnings or endings; the entire political calendar felt like one extended performance review broadcast on multiple channels, one endless audition for attention, outrage, and campaign donations. Debate, in the classical sense of structured reasoning about shared problems, had dissolved into content, something to be clipped and shared, measured in views rather than in wisdom. Citizens drifted from being participants to being audiences, consuming politics in the same posture with which they consumed everything else— scrolling, swiping, reacting. Government had not ceased to exist; it had drifted into gridlock and permanent improvisation, lurching from manufactured crisis to manufactured crisis while structural issues—aging infrastructure, demographic shifts, long-term economic imbalances—sat in the background like unaddressed medical conditions.

The United States was not unique in its strain. The European Union wrestled in 2025 with its own tensions between core and periphery, between member states demanding energy security and those insisting on climate discipline, between rural regions feeling left behind and metropolitan centers convinced they embodied the future. China, having spent decades fusing authoritarian control with economic ambition, now faced the complex task of sustaining growth under tightening global trade conditions and technological restrictions, while managing internal discontent that rarely made it onto official broadcasts. Russia leaned heavily on nostalgia, on the memory of past grandeur and wartime sacrifice, using aggression abroad to distract from stagnation at home.

Beyond formal states, technology giants and financial conglomerates behaved increasingly like empires without flags, commanding data instead of territory, issuing their own quasi-currencies in loyalty points and digital tokens, shaping speech and attention and even the boundaries of permissible debate through proprietary platforms whose rules citizens could not vote on and whose executives no one had elected.

The world did not operate on cooperation in any deep sense; it operated on ego—national ego, corporate ego, ideological ego—and ego, left unmanaged, is what ruins civilizations.

The warnings were not subtle. Scholars pointed to the drumbeat of reports released in early 2025—the trust surveys showing historic polarization and grievance, the global risk assessments listing conflict escalation, cyberwarfare, and climate shocks as converging threats, the humanitarian forecasts projecting hundreds of millions in need of aid—as indicators not simply of "a rough year," but of a system approaching its own limits. Yet the daily news cycle processed these alerts as content rather than as counsel. They trended for a day, sparked arguments for a weekend, and then vanished beneath the next wave of stimuli.

History's pattern, viewed honestly, is painfully consistent.

Once a society becomes too comfortable, it loses the instincts that built its greatness.

Once citizens become spectators instead of stakeholders, the nation begins to decay.

Once entertainment becomes more important than discipline, culture begins to weaken.

Once politics becomes performance, governance collapses into symbolism.

Once money becomes mostly symbolic, value becomes mostly imaginary.

Once people become deeply divided, the empire fractures internally long before any external enemy tests its borders.

These are not poetic generalizations. They are recurring timelines, written in different languages and under different banners, and in 2025 and 2026 they were repeating again, only this time with fiber-optic cables instead of messenger horses, with satellites instead of signal fires, with real-time feeds instead of town criers.

The most uncomfortable realization for anyone trained in history was that 2026 did not represent some strange anomaly—a bizarre outlier in an otherwise coherent narrative of progress—but a recognizable inflection point, the kind that appears again and again when an order has exhausted its underlying logic. The world had grown astonishingly capable in some domains—artificial intelligence, genomic science, logistics, real-time communication—while remaining astonishingly primitive in others—conflict resolution, equitable resource distribution, shared meaning, emotional maturity at scale.

There is a quieter truth that many historians admit to themselves, if not always in the polished language of journals. Empires do not collapse only because they grow weak; they collapse because they stop growing at all in the dimensions that matter.

They become obsessed with protecting what they have instead of building what comes next. They confuse preservation with progress, mistaking the defense of old arrangements for the creation of a better future. The imagination that once fueled their ascent gets replaced by a fear of loss, so that political energy turns inward, toward guarding privileges and symbols, while the rest of the world continues to move.

They become reactive instead of visionary, fearful instead of ambitious, rigid instead of adaptive—strategic on paper, chaotic in practice. Their institutions still speak the language of greatness, but their daily functioning revolves around survival: surviving the next election cycle, the next quarterly report, the next scandal, the next ratings dip, the next trending outrage.

By the time humanity stepped into 2026, this dynamic defined more than one capital city. Innovation raced ahead; governance limped behind. Code was deployed in days; treaties took years.

The tools existed to coordinate planetary responses to crises—pandemics, climate shocks, mass displacement—but the decision-making structures remained bound to national timelines and domestic political fears.

We had more access to information than any civilization in recorded history, and yet less agreement on basic reality. We had universities, think tanks, and research institutes generating sophisticated analysis, but fewer shared values underneath that knowledge and fewer shared definitions of what a "good society" should actually protect. Laws existed, often in great detail, but the cultural consensus that once gave them moral weight had eroded. There was measurable progress, but very little shared sense of direction.

The warning signs of imperial overextension were not hiding in archives; they were written into the news of 2025 and 2026: a coup in a small country no one in the global North could locate on a map without assistance, reminding observers how fragile institutions can be; a hastily negotiated peace deal in a long-suffering region that closed one chapter of violence while leaving another half-written; great-power tensions flaring over shipping lanes, semiconductors, and critical minerals; financial markets whipsawing on rumors of new tariffs, new sanctions, new default risks, new technological bans; heatwaves and floods displacing millions who had never contributed significantly to the emissions that destabilized their climate.

But empires, like individuals, rarely listen deeply when they are still standing. They hear the critique; they do not feel it as urgent. They assume that, because the roof has not yet fallen in, the soft sound of water in the walls can be safely ignored.

Collapse, however, is not only destruction. Collapse is revelation.

It shows what was real and what was merely performance.

It strips away illusions and reveals the difference between rhetoric and capacity.

It forces evolution on people and systems that would have chosen comfort indefinitely if comfort had remained an option.

Every empire that has fallen has also cleared space for something new: leaner, sharper, more aware, sometimes kinder, often at least more honest. The ashes become instruction. The ruins become curriculum. The mistakes become a blueprint labeled in negative space—this, at least, is what not to do again.

That is the part of the story popular culture often forgets, because endings are more dramatic than rebuilds. Collapse is not only an end. Collapse is also a reset.

2026, seen from a certain vantage point, was not just about the slow death of old empires—whether those empires were states, corporations, narratives, or ways of life. It was about the birth of new ones: new systems emerging in response to visible failure, new leaders learning to think in terms of networks rather than borders, new philosophies that treated consciousness and resilience as forms of power, new technologies that could either entrench control or distribute capability depending on who learned to wield them, new models of community less dependent on centralized permission and more grounded in local competence and global awareness.

The people who understood this did not spend all their energy clinging to what used to be, defending every existing structure as if it were sacred simply because it was familiar. They did not romanticize the old order while ignoring the damage it had already done. Instead, they did something harder and quieter. They studied the pattern with open eyes and admitted, without flattery, that the era they had grown up inside was ending.

They prepared, not in the survivalist sense of stockpiling canned goods and ammunition, but in the deeper sense of upgrading their own minds and capacities. They learned how systems actually worked—financial systems, technological systems, political systems, media systems—rather than accepting the simplified stories those systems told about themselves. They trained their attention to cut through noise. They practiced the discipline of staying informed without becoming consumed. They refused to let tribal loyalties, whether national or partisan or ideological, blind them to structural reality.

Those people were not simply passive observers in the narrow sense. They were Observers in the truest sense: individuals who used awareness as a form of agency, who treated seeing clearly as a moral responsibility, who understood that in a collapsing order, the only real safety is not in the illusion of stability but in the ability to evolve when that stability fails.

The echoes of old empires, heard more loudly in 2025 and 2026 than at any time in recent decades, were not solely warnings about destruction. They were, if one had the patience to listen, instructions for rebirth.

2026 was not the end of the world. It was the end of the world as it had been narrated to itself. Once that narration cracked, humanity no longer possessed the luxury of denial. The patterns were visible. The consequences were visible. The opportunities were visible to anyone willing to lift their eyes above the feed and look across time.

We were never meant to preserve the old indefinitely. We were meant to build the new. The difference, as 2026 made brutally clear, is that building the new requires first admitting what the old has become—and having the courage to step forward while the ceiling is still groaning, before it finally gives way.

CHAPTER 11

Crisis Breeds Innovators

Pressure does not just expose people. It creates them, stretches them, distorts them, and in a few rare cases tempers them into something so precise and unbreakable that later generations mistake their arrival for destiny instead of what it really was: a response to conditions everyone else tried not to look at too closely.

If you walk back through history with a clear, disciplined eye, you do not find civilization's turning points in the calm years, the tidy decades, the seasons when everyone felt reasonably safe and the headlines moved slowly enough for textbooks to keep up. You find them in the collision seasons, the years when the ground shook in ways that were obvious to some and "overblown" to others, the years when institutions faltered, systems failed in small but undeniable ways, and ordinary people were forced to decide whether they would cling to what they had been or become something else entirely.

The strongest leaders, the boldest creators, the most dangerous thinkers, the builders of new worlds are almost never children of comfort. They are children of disruption. They are forged in friction and loss, in uncertainty and grief, in the strange and disorienting in-between where the old world is dying in slow motion and the new world does not yet have a name, only a feeling.

By 2026, the entire planet had been dragged into that in-between. Humanity was not standing at the edge of a neat historical chapter break; it was stumbling through the middle of one. The world that had raised people in the 1990s, the 2000s, even the early 2010s, with its promises about education, employment, stability, and retirement, was not the world they were now living in. The social contract had not been officially ripped up, but the ink had faded, the signatures were suspect, and the fine print read differently in the harsh light of lived reality.

On the surface, it looked like chaos. Underneath, it was something far more precise. Old systems were being tested to failure, not in theory but in real time. Economic models that had held for generations began to buckle under the combined weight of aging populations, record debt, and technologies that could reprice an entire industry in a single product cycle. Political institutions in places like the United States and the European Union, long treated as anchors of the global order, revealed themselves as polarized, paralyzed, and unable to legislate at the speed of reality. Public trust in media, banking, healthcare, and government slid downward in a steady, visible line that even the most artful public relations could not hide.

The sense that "the center cannot hold" did not arrive as poetry. It arrived as mood: in the way people checked prices with a small, involuntary flinch; in the way executives spoke in private about risk while speaking in public about resilience; in the way parents stared at their children and quietly wondered what, exactly, they were handing off.

And yet the story did not begin in 2026. It rarely does in the year that gets the headline. The pressure that would define 2026 had been building quietly through 2024 and 2025, accumulating in decisions no one thought of as historic at the time.

In 2025, central banks around the world performed a kind of exhausted ballet, raising rates here, pausing there, improvising between inflation that refused to obey traditional models and markets that punished every move made in the wrong tone. Housing in major cities drifted further out of reach for ordinary earners. Corporate earnings calls began to list "AI integration" and "workforce optimization" as polite phrases for automation and layoffs. Labor strikes in logistics, healthcare, and education, from port workers in one hemisphere to nurses and teachers in another, signaled that whole sectors were no longer willing to carry systemic dysfunction silently.

The summer of 2025 brought a cascade of reminders that the planet itself was part of the story. Heat waves pushed infrastructure in major cities to the edge of failure. Drought on one continent collided with flooding on another. Insurance firms quietly rewrote their risk models while politicians continued to argue about language. A sprawling cyberattack in late 2025, aimed at a patchwork of regional utilities and hospital systems, did not collapse any one nation, but it did something more instructive: it showed, painfully and concretely, how thin the margin really was between functioning modern life and cascading disruption.

Behind closed doors, the current generation of leaders—presidents and prime ministers, central bankers and cabinet members, CEOs and board chairs—felt that pressure in ways they rarely admitted out loud. Many were not afraid of the abstract future; they were afraid of being exposed in the present. They had spent entire careers mastering a certain script: how to speak in markets 'language, how to calm investors, how to win elections, how to manage quarterly expectations. That script had been written for a slower world.

Now they found themselves sitting in briefings about generative AI systems that could draft laws faster than legislatures, design products faster than R&D divisions, and destabilize labor markets faster than any policy could repair. They listened to security teams describe threat surfaces that spanned not just borders and oceans, but code libraries, model weights, and cloud architectures controlled by other corporations entirely. They watched as a viral post, a synthetic video, or a coordinated swarm of bots could move public opinion more in twelve hours than months of carefully crafted messaging.

In private, some admitted what they would never say on record: they did not fully understand the tools being deployed in their own name. They signed off on AI task forces and digital transformation strategies, on supply-chain rewiring and ESG adjustments, but at three in the morning many of them were reading briefs written by people twenty years younger and praying they were not missing something essential.

Fear leaked out in odd ways. In the way senior executives dismissed young builders as "naïve" while quietly hiring consultants to explain the very technologies those builders were using. In the way veteran politicians mocked online organizers even as their campaigns scrambled to reverse engineer the same tactics. In the way legacy media outlets derided independent creators for "lacking standards" even as they tracked, with obsessive detail, how many millions of people were no longer getting their information from traditional channels at all.

Leadership was not only under pressure. It was exposed. Titles, offices, corner suites, and motorcades could no longer mask a simple fact visible to anyone paying attention in 2025: many of the people in charge had been trained to manage stability, not transformation. They were fluent in the language of a world that was already gone.

While this was happening at the visible top, 2025 was doing something quieter at the edges. It was shaping a different kind of person in the background.

In apartments, co-working spaces, garages, and borrowed corners of corporate time, individuals who felt the unease of the decade began to experiment. A freight broker in Kansas City built a small AI tool to predict pricing volatility and discovered it could see patterns their carrier partners never mentioned. A laid-off designer in London used generative systems to prototype three product ideas in the time it used to take to fully mock up one and stumbled into a niche business that served thousands directly online. A teacher in Lagos cobbled together open-source tools to run a micro-schooling platform that reached students far beyond her neighborhood.

They were not yet "leaders" in any official sense. They did not have titles or think-tank profiles. In 2025, most of them would not even have called themselves innovators. They were simply people who were unwilling to wait for someone else to fix the world around them. Pressure turned into curiosity. Curiosity turned into practice. Practice turned into competence.

By the time 2026 arrived, those experiments were no longer prototypes on private hard drives. They were live systems. Subscriptions. Products. Movements. Communities. And the contrast between those emerging architectures and the visibly straining legacy systems became too stark for anyone with clear sight to miss.

Crisis is rarely symmetrical. The same pressure that crushes some people compresses others into something unbreakable. The same fire that melts old structures hardens certain individuals into steel. That is what 2026 did. It separated spectators from architects. It separated those waiting to be rescued from those who had quietly been building lifeboats since the uneasy months of 2025.

The people who rose that year were not blind to the chaos. They simply read it differently. While most people looked at the red flashing indicators—currency jitters, climate emergencies, contested elections, automation waves—and thought, this is the end, they looked at the same dashboard and thought, this is the opening.

Every failing system was more than a tragedy. It was an x-ray. It revealed structure. It made vulnerabilities visible. It showed, with painful clarity, where something new had to be built if civilization was going to be anything more than a museum of past strength.

Every industry shaking on its foundations was not just a risk. It was space. A sign that incumbent players had lost their monopoly on competence. A sign that new entrants could step in, not with incremental tweaks, but with fundamentally different assumptions about how value could move.

Every institution losing legitimacy was not just a sign of decline. It was a vacancy sign hung over the very idea of leadership. If the old authorities no longer commanded automatic trust, someone else would have to earn it, and earning it in 2026 did not mean mastering the script of a press conference. It meant the ability to build systems that worked when older systems did not.

To most of the world, 2026 was a barrage. Headlines, alerts, emergencies. A heat dome here, a banking scare there, an election crisis somewhere else, rolling labor disruptions, new AI releases, new cyber incidents, new diplomatic standoffs. It was exhausting simply to stay informed, and many people, understandably, stopped trying.

The innovators could not afford to stop. They experienced 2026 as data. They did not deny the fear or the fatigue—they felt it like everyone else—but they refused to stop at the feeling. They asked sharper questions. They let discomfort sit long enough for pattern to emerge. Where the average citizen saw "everything is falling apart," they saw "this particular system is failing for these particular reasons, in this particular sequence, which means it can be replaced, re-routed, or redesigned."

When artificial intelligence swept through offices, warehouses, studios, and support centers, millions of workers felt an existential threat. They saw tasks migrate from human hands to systems. They watched departments "restructured" after yet another proof-of-concept demo. They read think pieces about the end of work and quietly wondered what would be left for them.

The innovators felt the same tremor. They simply followed it in a different direction. They saw that if a machine could handle the repetitive, the predictable, and the mechanically complex, then human energy could finally be redirected toward what machines could not yet do: deep design, creative synthesis, nuanced relationship, contextual judgment, moral decision-making. They recognized that one person, armed with intelligent tools, could now create what once required an entire team, and that the question was not "How do I protect my old job description?" but "How do I become the kind of person who directs this new power instead of being displaced by it?"

When supply chains snarled and everyday products turned unpredictable, most households felt only frustration. They saw empty shelves, delayed deliveries, and rising fees and responded with a vocabulary of complaint: broken, incompetent, rigged. Innovators saw something else entirely: dependency charts, single points of failure hidden in plain sight, opportunities for regional networks, parallel distribution routes, new manufacturing hubs, and more resilient ways of moving goods. They understood that whoever could reduce volatility in a volatile world would not only be profitable. They would become indispensable.

When currencies eroded and the concept of "saving for later" looked weaker by the month, the average response was anger or resignation. People raged online or tuned out entirely. Innovators did something harder and far less glamorous. They learned. They studied how value actually moved in a world of unstable fiat, digital assets, programmable money, platform tokens, and shifting regulations. They experimented with instruments most people dismissed as "too risky" or "too complicated" until they understood them from the inside out.

When political institutions descended further into televised performance and permanent campaign mode, when 2025's endless hearings and 2026's election storms blurred together into one long show, many citizens treated it as tragic theater—something to be watched with cynicism or ignored in exhaustion. Innovators saw the vacuum underneath. They recognized that if the old gatekeepers were distracted by their own reflections, there was room to build new forms of governance at smaller scales: local coordination platforms, neighborhood mutual-aid networks, parallel education systems, new kinds of cooperatives, new channels of influence that did not require anyone's permission to exist.

When entertainment and outrage fused into a 24-hour spectacle and people numbed themselves into submission, innovators saw an opening in the opposite direction. They realized that in a culture of distraction, depth would stand out; in a culture where everyone was selling escape, anyone who built tools for engagement with reality would be rare. Attention, they understood, could be earned not only by amplifying noise, but by offering clarity.

When the psychological crash finally surfaced and people admitted how broken they felt—after years of pretending they were "fine," after the silent breakdowns of 2024 and the masked burnouts of 2025—innovators saw more than personal tragedy. They saw a massive, underserved need for frameworks, spaces, technologies, and communities that helped human beings adapt to an accelerating world without losing their minds.

The pattern was not subtle. Innovators do not run from problems. They interrogate them. They turn a problem over in their hands until the shape of a solution begins to show through the cracks. They know that the bigger the problem, the greater the leverage if they solve even one crucial piece of it.

And all the while, the old leaders watched. Some with contempt, some with curiosity, many with a tightness behind the eyes that did not make it into official portraits. They were scared not only of losing control, but of being revealed as out of their depth. Their greatest fear was not that the world was changing—that had always been true—but that it was changing in ways for which their training had not prepared them, while people with no titles, no pedigree, and no institutional backing were somehow more fluent in the language of the new age.

2026 drew a line with surgical precision. On one side were the sleepers: those waiting for someone else to fix it, waiting for the "right" leader or the "right" policy, waiting for the market to "bounce back," waiting for the old comfort to quietly return as if it had ever been more than a temporary condition. They clung to old identities—job titles, degrees, affiliations—even as those labels stopped matching the terrain around them.

On the other side were the awake: those who understood, often because 2025 had already humbled them, that the world might never calm down in the way their parents had described, and that the only realistic question was not "When will this end?" but "Who do I need to become so I can operate in a world that may stay this volatile for the rest of my life?" They were willing to become beginners again, even in midlife. They were willing to learn new tools, enter new domains, abandon respectability long enough to become effective.

The sleepers treated artificial intelligence as an enemy to fear, complain about, or ignore. The awake treated it as leverage, something to be mapped and mastered. The sleepers drowned in entertainment. The awake cut their consumption nearly in half and redirected that time toward building. The sleepers fought each other along increasingly narrow ideological lines. The awake found each other across geography, race, class, and background, forming small, dense alliances bound not by slogans, but by shared commitment to create systems that would still matter ten years later.

Crisis did not pick winners. People picked their stance toward the crisis.

Most of the true innovators of 2026 did not look like legends at the time. They did not broadcast every step because they were too busy doing the work. They were not building for likes or applause. They were building because they could not look at the collapsing scaffolding of the old world and do nothing. They stared at the same broken charts as everyone else, but their last question was different. Not only, what is happening to us, but what is opening because this is happening.

The world did not need more of the old leaders, whose authority depended on structures visibly wearing out. It did not need more institutions obsessed with defending their status instead of fulfilling their purpose. It did not need more politicians whose primary skill was surviving the news cycle or more outlets optimized for attention rather than accuracy.

The world needed people who could read the new terrain. People who could think faster without becoming reckless, adapt faster without becoming unmoored, see deeper than the surface narrative, build smarter than the systems they were replacing, command advanced tools without being commanded by them, speak with honesty in rooms full of performance, create solutions where others only traded complaints, lead without waiting for a job title, and influence without resorting to manipulation.

They understood that the future is not something that arrives evenly distributed like a weather pattern. It is something that is designed, often by a relatively small number of people who are willing to stay awake while everyone else is sedating themselves. And design, in every era, begins with disruption.

2026 did not reward comfort. Comfort was one of the first casualties. It rewarded courage instead. It did not reward memorization of old answers. It rewarded the capacity to generate new ones under pressure. It did not reward imitation of past success formulas. It rewarded the willingness to write new formulas in environments where failure was visible and stakes were high. It did not reward clinging to rules written for a different century. It rewarded those honest enough to recognize when the rules themselves had quietly expired.

Crisis did not destroy opportunity. It concentrated it into fewer hands. The open question was whose hands those would be.

The innovators of 2026 were not superhuman. They were not immune to fear or exhaustion. They felt the same tiredness, the same doubt, the same grief as everyone else. The difference was what they did with it. Under pressure that fractured many, they allowed themselves to be compressed into focus. Under uncertainty that paralyzed others, they took small, relentless steps. Under a collapsing world, they chose to become builders of the next one.

The old world did not vanish in a single dramatic instant. It sagged, splintered, and finally gave way in a series of visible and invisible breaks. The new world did not appear in an announcement. It began quietly—in small apartments and borrowed offices, in notebooks and code repositories, in voice notes recorded after midnight and shared with one other person who understood. It began in conversations between people who had every reason to give up and chose, stubbornly, not to.

It began in the hearts and minds of people who accepted a hard truth: if everything is going to change, someone is going to decide what it changes into.

2025 softened the ground. 2026 drew the line. And the ones who stepped across it, the ones who refused to outsource their responsibility to some hypothetical savior, stopped waiting for that someone and became it.

CHAPTER 12

The Observer

In every collapsing age, a new kind of human begins to emerge from the background, almost unnoticed at first, not because they are louder or richer or draped in visible power, but because in a time when most eyes are dazzled or dulled, they retain the most endangered capacity of all – the ability to actually see.

In 2025, before the word "collision" had attached itself to the year ahead, the training ground for this new human was already being prepared in plain sight. The headlines told one story – another election cycle spiraling into performance, another spike in inflation dismissed as "temporary," another ceasefire broken in a war that had already fallen out of fashion in the feeds, another AI breakthrough announced as progress while quietly erasing whole categories of work – but beneath those stories, there was a different text, written in quiet layoffs, in shrinking savings, in increasingly fragile supply chains, in nervous glances between executives who repeated the word "resilient" while their own eyes betrayed doubt.

Most people did what most people always do when the world begins to tilt and no one wants to admit it. They picked a side in the argument rather than a position in the reality. They clung harder to their preferred news sources, doubled down on their talking points, refreshed their feeds, chose leaders to hate and leaders to worship, and called the whole pattern "being informed," even as their inner world grew more brittle by the month.

The Observer moved through the same year, under the same sky and inside the same networks, but they inhabited it differently.

They felt the same tremors: the rolling bank scares that briefly made depositors wonder if their money actually existed; the blackout in a European city traced to a "software fault" that sounded, to anyone listening closely, more like a successful test of someone's cyber capabilities; the viral deepfake of a world leader that remained online for hours before any official correction landed; the quiet memo in a mid-level office announcing that "AI augmentation" would require a restructuring of staff. They did not feel less fear in the face of these events. They simply refused to let fear be the final author of their conclusions.

Where others rushed to anesthetize their unease with more noise, the Observer did something almost subversive for the age. They created space inside themselves.

They allowed the discomfort to sit there, undistracted, long enough to form questions.

What is this really showing me.

Who benefits if everyone stays confused at this exact moment.

What pattern connects this election, this software "glitch," this supply disruption, this sudden new law, this trending outrage.

In 2025, reaction had become the default posture of the human animal. A notification chimed and the nervous system jumped. A headline flared and emotions spiked. A clip went viral and opinions formed on command. People lived like exposed wires, sparking at every touch.

The Observer began, very deliberately, to insert a thin layer of distance between the touch and the spark. A pause measured not in minutes, but in intention.

That pause was their first act of rebellion.

In that pause, they noticed that the language used to describe events often mattered more than the events themselves. They watched how a banking scare became a "temporary liquidity issue," how a censorship decision became "content moderation," how economic pain became "necessary adjustment," how increased monitoring became "enhanced safety," how another round of layoffs became "strategic realignment." They listened to the adjectives as much as to the nouns, hearing in each choice of phrasing an attempt not merely to describe reality but to shape the acceptable response to it.

Where the average citizen consumed the headline and moved on, the Observer quietly asked: Why this word, now, in this context, from this mouth.

The difference seems small on the surface. In practice, it was the line dividing those who would be carried into 2026 unconscious and those who would step into it awake.

Observers were not, as the myths of genius would like to claim, born with some exotic extra sense. In 2025 they walked factory floors, answered calls in overwhelmed hospitals, coded late at night for companies that would reorganize without warning, sat through meetings in logistics firms watching spreadsheets strain under shipping delays, taught in classrooms where students' eyes flickered constantly toward their screens, preached in congregations split by politics, and fixed trucks, hairlines, servers, marriages, and supply routes in a world that insisted everything was fine as long as the stadiums stayed full and the streams kept loading.

Their difference was not their occupation. It was their discipline.

They treated their attention as an asset instead of a toy.

While most people surrendered their cognitive bandwidth in tiny increments – one more scroll, one more video, one more argument with a stranger – the Observer began to account for theirs. They noticed how they felt after an hour lost in outrage and how they felt after an hour spent tracing cause and effect. They noticed how their judgment clouded after consuming twenty stories in twenty minutes and how clarity returned when they sat with one story long enough to see the system behind it.

Attention, for them, was no longer merely a reaction to outside demand. It became a chosen direction.

By the time 2026 arrived with its stacked crises and visible fractures, this practice had already reshaped the Observer's inner landscape. The same barrage that left others dizzy – another extreme weather event, another currency scare, another geopolitical escalation, another AI model announced while the last one's impacts were still being understood – struck the Observer as data rather than pure threat. Not because they were naïve about the danger, but because they had trained themselves, in the slower burn of 2025, to look first for structure.

They saw how a conflict in one region translated almost immediately into fuel prices in another, which translated into food prices in a third, which translated into quiet desperation in the face of a rising grocery bill in a fourth. They watched how a change in a social media algorithm shifted not just what trended, but which protests received attention and which did not, which catastrophes felt "real" to the public and which remained invisible even as they unfolded. They noticed how each new artificial intelligence "assistant" came with a new set of terms and conditions, a new data stream, a new opportunity to train systems that would later be deployed in ways users had not foreseen.

Where most saw isolated storms, the Observer saw a single atmosphere.

They understood that what was marketed as separate crises – a mental health epidemic here, a political crisis there, an economic "adjustment" over there, a climate emergency in another quadrant – were, in practice, expressions of the same over-clocked civilization hitting its limits.

This understanding did not make them immune to fatigue. If anything, it deepened their grief. But it also hardened their resolve.

In a year when leaders in many sectors were revealed as smaller than their titles – presidents who staged performance while quietly outpaced by events, CEOs caught flat-footed by technologies they had hyped for shareholders, generals forced to admit that war had moved into domains for which their training had not prepared them, media figures more dependent on engagement metrics than on accuracy – the Observer saw clearly why the old archetype of leadership was afraid.

Those leaders had been formed in a world where control could be maintained by managing information and gatekeeping access. In the compressed environment of 2025–2026, information flowed too fast to manage cleanly, and gatekeeping had been partially automated away. The rituals that once conferred authority – the press conference, the televised address, the carefully staged summit – now landed inside a population that could fact-check in real time, cross-reference across borders, and replay every contradiction.

Power, in that light, began to look less like a podium and more like an ability: the ability to interpret patterns faster than they formed, to adjust without disintegrating, to hold one's mind steady without outsourcing judgment to the loudest source.

That ability is precisely what the Observer had been cultivating while others were still rehearsing their talking points.

This is why Observers are dangerous to brittle systems.

You cannot easily scare someone who has already spent a year staring directly at the conditions others refuse to name. You cannot cheaply bribe someone who has already measured the cost of comfort against the price of clarity. You cannot herd someone whose first instinct, when confronted with a stampede, is to ask where the stampede is being directed and why.

By mid-2026, the world could be roughly divided into two kinds of consciousness, though no census would ever record it that way. On one side were those whose identities had fused completely with their roles inside the old order – job titles, party affiliations, brand allegiances, familiar scripts. When those roles began to lose their footing, the people inside them did too. Their sense of self rose and fell with indices and approval ratings they did not control.

On the other side were the Observers. They still had jobs, loyalties, preferences, beliefs, and fears. But beneath those surface layers they had been slowly, sometimes painfully, building another foundation: an identity rooted not in a single institution, but in their capacity to remain awake inside any institution; not in a single narrative, but in their commitment to track reality even when it embarrassed their narrative; not in a single comfort, but in their willingness to tolerate discomfort as the price of seeing clearly.

The Observer's life, from the outside, did not always look dramatic. You might pass them on a crowded subway in 2026 and see only someone reading an article to the end instead of skimming the headline. You might work beside them in a warehouse and notice only that they understood the flow of freight two steps beyond what the computer screen showed. You might see them in a tense family conversation and notice that, when everyone else reached for slogans, they reached for questions.

But if you followed them quietly through that year, you would see a pattern.

They turned down some forms of entertainment not because entertainment is evil, but because they understood that attention spent numbing cannot also be spent noticing.

They listened to people they disagreed with not to be converted, but to map out the emotional landscape that bad actors would later exploit.

They learned how the tools of the new age actually worked — not just AI and finance and logistics and digital media, but the tools of their own psychology. They studied their own triggers, their own biases, their own narratives, precisely so those vulnerabilities could not be turned so easily into levers.

They took seriously the boring things others postponed: sleep, nutrition, a quiet walk without headphones, a notebook instead of another app, an honest inventory of what they actually believed when no one was watching.

These habits did not make the world less chaotic. They made the Observer less hostage to that chaos.

History will eventually portray 2026 as a year of spectacular events — the charts and graphs, the conflicts and collapses — because that is how textbooks simplify trauma. But the real pivot did not happen in legislatures or trading floors alone. It happened in millions of private decisions made by people who had been tempered by 2025's unease and chose, in 2026, not to anesthetize themselves any further.

They chose to remain conscious in a time when unconsciousness was being marketed as self-care.

They chose to hold their attention in a time when attention was the most contested resource on the planet.

They chose to keep asking, "What is really happening here, beneath the performance," in a time when performance had almost completely replaced reality.

Those choices did not come with medals or hashtags. They came with a different reward: orientation.

When systems lurched, Observers did not flail in every direction at once. When narratives flipped, they did not need to reinvent themselves from scratch. When the old empires of thought and finance and governance began to creak under their own contradictions, Observers were already standing on ground that did not depend entirely on any one of them.

The world that followed 2026 would still be unstable, still contested, still unfinished. But the balance of power within it would tilt, quietly but decisively, toward those who had learned how to see.

Not those who shouted the most about being "awake," but those who had done the daily, unglamorous labor of staying awake.

Not those who built brands around dissent, but those who cultivated discernment.

Not those who merely suspected manipulation, but those who could map it, name it, and navigate through it without becoming consumed by hatred.

The Observer is that human.

Not mythic. Not invincible. Not exempt from the pain of a shifting age.

Simply someone who decides, again and again, that in a world accelerating toward collision, the most radical act is not to run faster with the crowd, but to step half a pace back, lift their eyes above the dust, and insist on seeing where, and what, and who all this motion is truly for.

PART ONE:

When The Old World Hit Its Limit

CHAPTER 13

The Shift Year

Every era has a year that, at the time, feels almost ordinary—a handful of headlines, a few spikes of panic, the usual calendar of holidays and routines—and yet when historians return to it with the distance of decades, they circle it in red and write in the margin, "Here. This is where the line bent." The strange thing about those hinge years is that they never arrive looking like hinges. They arrive looking like Tuesdays. Traffic jams. Grocery lists. Phone screens. That was 2026—except 2026 did not fall from a clear blue sky. It was not a surprise guest. It was the final, inevitable chapter in a story that had been accelerating quietly since at least 2017, a story most people thought of as "normal life."

To understand why 2026 felt like a rupture, you have to walk back through the years that pretended to be stable while the floor under them was already cracking.

In 2017, the phrase "post-truth" shifted from clever commentary to operating condition. Politics in the United States and beyond turned into a permanent fever, a contest not over policy but over reality itself. Social media platforms, which had once been marketed as tools for connection, revealed themselves as enormous attention markets, their invisible currencies outrage, fear, and validation. Algorithms learned that the shortest route to engagement was division, and so they fed people the digital equivalents of sugar and gasoline: content that confirmed their beliefs and inflamed their resentments.

The years that followed—2018, 2019—blurred into a strange prelude. Economies grew on paper. Markets climbed. New apps launched. Phones improved. Streaming multiplied. Yet beneath the graphs and product releases, something subtle shifted in the collective nervous system. People spoke more about burnout though they slept less. News cycles compressed from days into hours. Scandals that would once have dominated a season now burned out in a long weekend. Attention became a resource constantly under siege, and while few could yet articulate it, the capacity to think in long arcs was already being eroded by the constant demand to react in short bursts.

Then came 2020.

If 2017–2019 were the tremors, 2020 was the first visible crack in the wall. A virus crossed borders faster than most governments could process the first briefings. Cities fell still. Planes sat idle. Supply chains—those hidden circulatory systems of global life—shuddered, then lurched, then seized in certain places. For a brief moment, the world experienced something ancient and forgotten: a unified interruption. Everyone, from billionaires to hourly workers, discovered that the normal they had trusted could be halted by something they could not even see.

The pandemic did many things at once. It exposed how fragile national health systems really were. It revealed which work was "essential" and how poorly it was usually paid. It compressed ten years of digital adoption into eighteen months, driving schooling, therapy, meetings, funerals, and friendships onto screens. It left a residue of grief and disorientation that would not be measured only in bodies lost, but in trust eroded and expectations quietly shattered.

2021 arrived not as a fresh beginning but as a long exhale that never quite finished. Vaccines spread, but so did misinformation. Lockdowns eased, but the nervous habits remained. People spoke about "getting back to normal," yet normal no longer fit. Workers began to resign from jobs that had once seemed safe, not because they had clear alternatives, but because the previous bargain—sacrifice your time, health, and presence in exchange for stability—had been revealed as a fragile myth. The phrase "The Great Resignation" tried to capture something deeper: a widespread refusal to return to a life that had quietly been hollowing people out.

In 2022, war returned to Europe in a way many had thought consigned to history. Tanks rolled, cities were shelled, millions fled across borders with suitcases and phone chargers, and the global order, which had for decades treated certain conflicts as distant brush fires, suddenly remembered that large-scale invasion was not a relic. Energy markets convulsed. Grain shipments stalled. Nations discovered that the stability of their own households was bound to decisions made in distant capitals they had only half watched before.

That same year and into 2023, inflation crept from abstract graphs into kitchen tables. Groceries, rent, fuel, utilities—all rose faster than wages that had already been stagnant for years. People found themselves running harder just to stand in the same place, and the anger that followed did not know where to land. Governments blamed supply chains and geopolitical shocks. Central banks played with interest rates like levers in a failing machine. Corporations raised prices and issued record profits. Workers felt squeezed between stories that did not match their receipts.

Then, in late 2022 and across 2023, another force stepped into the spotlight: general-purpose artificial intelligence. Systems that could write, code, pass exams, generate images, and imitate voices moved from research labs into browsers and phones. For some, these systems felt like miracles—tireless collaborators that could answer questions and draft documents on command. For others, they felt like quiet assassins stalking their livelihoods, capable of doing in seconds what had taken them years to learn. Either way, a line had been crossed. Intelligence, or something convincingly like it, had become a commodity.

By 2024, the world was running at a speed that its institutions could not match. Wars persisted and multiplied in both physical and digital space. Climate disruption showed itself in longer fire seasons, heavier floods, stranger storms. Election cycles, especially in the United States, blurred into a continuous campaign that never really ended. Trust in media, government, and expertise slid steadily downward. People were not merely skeptical. They were exhausted.

And then, on an April afternoon, the sky itself participated.

On April 8, 2024, a total solar eclipse crossed North America. In cities and fields, on highways and in schoolyards, millions of people stood outside and watched daylight collapse into an unnatural twilight. Streetlights flickered on at midday. Birds fell silent or circled in confusion. For a few minutes in the path of totality, the sun became a black disc ringed with fire, and the ordinary world—the emails, the errands, the endless notifications—fell completely away.

Most treated it as a spectacle, a beautiful rarity. But for many who were already attuned to the deeper unease of the age, it felt like something else: a rehearsal in the sky, a symbolic preview of what it meant for the familiar light to vanish and a stranger kind of darkness to reveal the hidden corona around it. A brief, cosmic reminder that the sources of our certainty can be obscured in an instant, and that when they are, we see structures and forces that daylight had concealed.

2024 did not end with that eclipse, of course. The year carried on, as years do. Markets rallied and dipped. Conflicts flared and cooled. A new generation of AI models rolled out with better language, sharper images, deeper integration into work and governance. The cost of living continued its slow, grinding ascent. Elections around the world intensified the sense that politics had become less about direction and more about survival. Yet under all the noise, a growing number of people felt it in their bones: the old world had used up its margin.

2025 became the year of attempted reassurance. Narratives shifted to the language of "soft landings" and "temporary volatility." Companies spoke of "right-sizing" rather than layoffs. Governments promised that inflation would ease, that conflicts would stabilize, that new technologies would be harnessed responsibly. In some places, there were moments of genuine progress. In others, the gap between official calm and lived reality widened to the point of absurdity.

Hospitals struggled with staffing even as demand for care grew. Teachers faced classrooms full of students whose attention had been silently rewired by years of algorithmic stimuli. Freight networks pretended at normalcy while operating with little slack and aging infrastructure. Entire professions began to realize that their job descriptions were quietly becoming training data. The people who would later be recognized as the innovators and Observers of 2026 were, in 2025, still largely invisible—burning out in middle management, freelancing between contracts, experimenting with side projects at night, reading the signs and understanding, if only privately, that there would be no return to the world that had raised them.

By the time 2026 arrived, the stage was not just set; it was overloaded.

It did not announce itself with a single catastrophe. There was no neat "before and after" line that could be drawn through one event on the evening news. The old world did not end with a meteor or a declaration. It ended with a layered, collective realization that what people had been calling "normal" for the previous decade was not normal at all—it was an unsustainable moment extended past its natural lifespan.

For years, the global system had been running beyond its design. Economies had been stretched past sustainability by debt, speculation, and the assumption of endless growth. Politics had been stretched past trust by permanent campaigns and weaponized identity. Technology had been stretched past comprehension by tools whose consequences no one fully understood before deploying them. Human psychology had been stretched past its limits by the demand to process planetary crises in real time while still handling rent, relationships, and groceries.

2026 was not when the damage began. It was when the bill came due.

People tried, at first, to frame it as another rough patch. They blamed unpopular leaders. They blamed one central bank, one corporation, one party, one conflict. It was more comfortable to search for a villain than to admit that the entire operating pattern was misaligned. But patterns, once seen, do not unsee themselves.

By 2026, the war fronts that had once been distant and occasional were constant and strangely ambient. Citizens woke to news of drones hitting logistics hubs thousands of miles away, only to feel the echo weeks later in price spikes at their local store. Cyber operations targeted power grids, hospitals, shipping software. Conflict no longer respected borders or war declarations; it moved through code and signal. "Front lines" now meant server racks, satellite constellations, critical databases, and the attention of entire populations.

The economy, already feverish, began to behave less like a set of rational markets and more like an exhausted organism fighting itself. Prices rose and fell in waves that felt disconnected from any ordinary explanation. Wages, for most, still lagged behind the cost of existing. Savings accounts that had taken years to build melted under the combined heat of inflation and instability. The quiet assumption that had underpinned the twentieth-century economic story—that if you worked hard and followed the rules, the system would more or less protect you—finally broke in a way that even the most optimistic could not ignore.

At the same time, money itself changed texture. Governments moved forward with digital currencies that promised frictionless transactions and real-time oversight. Crypto markets oscillated between scandal, regulation, reinvention, and renewed speculation. Ordinary people, who might once have considered "value" a fixed property of paper, metal, or a number on a bank app, found themselves wrestling with a harder truth: value was not a law of nature. It was an agreement. And the agreement was under renegotiation.

Beneath the surface of war and economics, the inner lives of millions reached a breaking point. By 2026, humanity's nervous system had been living under near-constant bombardment for almost a decade—political crises, pandemics, social movements, economic shocks, climate emergencies, technological leaps— each one demanding attention, judgment, and emotional processing. The result was not just stress; it was erosion of the basic capacities that make a mind feel like a livable place.

People began to describe their experience with new language. They were not only tired. They were emptied. Not only anxious. They were disoriented. Not only sad. They were unmoored from any coherent narrative about who they were and where their lives were going. Burnout statistics rose, but even those metrics felt shallow compared to what was actually unfolding: a widespread loss of inner architecture.

In earlier centuries, such a crisis of meaning might have been localized to a particular class or region. In 2026, it was synchronized by networks. The same viral clip that triggered outrage in one country sparked fatigue in another and dark humor in a third, all in the same hour. The same economic shock echoed in currencies, markets, and household budgets around the globe. People in very different cultures found themselves sending the same late-night messages, framed in different words but carrying the same confession:

"I do not know how to live in this world as it is currently arranged."

As minds frayed, entertainment finished its transformation into anesthesia. Streaming platforms trained people to consume narrative in long, numbing marathons. Short-form video trained them to expect emotional stimulation in sub-ten-second bursts. AI-generated content flooded feeds with endless variations of what people had already proven they would watch. The point was no longer to offer stories worth remembering. It was to offer distractions sufficient to delay reflection.

Politics, instead of offering orientation, devolved fully into spectacle. Leaders discovered that clips of confrontation traveled further than careful explanations, that anger mobilized faster than nuance, that being "on brand" mattered more than being accurate. Citizens, already psychologically exhausted, retreated into curated tribes where they could outsource thinking to group narratives that did their feeling for them. Public discourse ceased to be a search for shared reality and became, instead, a competition between incompatible storylines.

Meanwhile, the literal machinery of civilization—ports, roads, rails, power grids, water systems—labored under pressure they were not designed to bear. Supply chains, optimized for speed and efficiency rather than resilience, struggled to recover from one disruption before the next arrived. A storm here, a labor dispute there, a conflict over there, a software failure somewhere else, and suddenly entire regions found themselves short of basics they had assumed would always be available. The hidden complexity of "just in time" logistics became visible the moment "just in time" failed.

Seen from one angle, 2026 looked like simultaneous crisis in every direction.

Seen from another, more sober angle, it looked like something else: correction.

When a body runs a fever long enough, either the immune system reasserts control or the organism collapses. When a market inflates asset prices far beyond their underlying value, eventually the prices fall back to reality or the system crashes. When a bridge is asked to bear more weight than its engineers accounted for, the structure either holds by grace of hidden strength or it fails and the failure exposes every miscalculation embedded in its design.

Correction is not revenge. It is reality reasserting itself over fantasy.

2026 was reality reasserting itself over almost a decade of wishful thinking, deferred maintenance, ideological self-hypnosis, and technological acceleration without ethical traction. The wars that "no one could have predicted" were, in fact, predictable outcomes of unresolved tensions. The divisions that "suddenly appeared" had been cultivated for years by profit models that rewarded polarization. The inflation that "came out of nowhere" was the visible manifestation of choices that had seemed painless when they were first made. The psychological crash that "no one saw coming" was preceded by years of constant stimulation and dwindling space for reflection.

Humanity had spent the years from roughly 2017 to 2025 building speed without direction, layering complexity without redundancy, amplifying voices without deepening wisdom. In 2026, the curve arrived.

Every civilization reaches such a line—a threshold beyond which its inherited ways of thinking, governing, earning, and relating can no longer carry the weight they are asked to bear. In earlier centuries, that threshold might have manifested as a revolution in one kingdom, a famine in another, a banking collapse in a third. In the hyper connected world of the early twenty-first century, it manifested everywhere at once.

That is what made 2026 the Shift Year.

It was not the bloodiest year on record. It was not the one with the single worst headline. It was, instead, the year in which clarity finally outpaced denial. A year in which enough people, across enough domains, looked at the pattern and admitted that "normal" was not an option waiting patiently on the other side of a few reforms. The old world was not having a bad season. It was finished in its current form.

That recognition carried a brutal implication. If the old pattern was over, then the instinct to "get back" to it was not merely misguided; it was dangerous. Nostalgia became a liability—a way of clinging to structures that could no longer protect anyone. Minor adjustments to broken systems began to look less like pragmatism and more like anesthesia.

By the end of 2026, those who were paying true attention— those emerging Observers and innovators—felt a different question settle into their lives. Instead of asking, "When will this storm pass so we can rebuild what we had," they began to ask, "What must be built now that cannot be built under the old assumptions at all."

The world had reached a hinge.

On one side of that hinge lay the exhausted dream that the old arrangements could be patched, painted, and sold back to a weary public as "stability." On the other side lay a harsher but more honest path: accepting that the old story had hit its limit, and that whatever came next would not be a restoration but a redesign.

The Shift Year did not answer which path humanity would ultimately choose. It did something more subtle and more permanent. It made the choice visible.

143

THE SHIFT YEAR

PART TWO:
The Rise of Architects

When a civilization finally collides with its own limits, history does not merely record the inventory of what cracked, collapsed, or could no longer stand under its own weight; it records, with far more precision and far more cruelty, the men and women who adjusted their inner architecture fast enough to survive the tilt, those who refused to pretend that the old scaffolding still held, and who, in the middle of the dust and noise, began quietly drafting blueprints for something that did not yet have a name.

For most people living through 2026, adaptation did not arrive as a heroic announcement or a cinematic moment of resolve; it arrived as a series of small, deeply inconvenient choices—about what to look at and what to ignore, about which work to cling to and which to release, about which allegiances were inherited and which were earned, about which beliefs still held weight and which had become sentimental habits, about whether the story of self they had been repeating for years could still survive contact with reality. Those choices felt personal and private in the moment—an extra hour of study, a difficult conversation, a quiet refusal to scroll, a risky email sent at midnight—but taken together, they had civilizational consequences.

The Shift Year did not redraw the world along the familiar lines that textbooks love to categorize—class, race, geography, party, flag; those lines still existed, still mattered, still hurt—but they were no longer the decisive coordinates. The line that really mattered ran invisibly through every country and cut every demographic, tracing itself through households and group chats, boardrooms and break rooms, temples and timelines. It did not separate rich from poor, urban from rural, or left from right; it separated ways of being.

Those who insisted on sleeping with their eyes open from those who agreed, however reluctantly, to stay awake.

Those who hardened into rigid self-definitions from those who allowed themselves to become adaptive organisms in an unstable environment.

Those who drowned in stimuli and called it awareness from those who learned to observe without being devoured.

On one side of that line stood the restorers of the old story. They spent 2026 trying to resuscitate a world that was already signing its own discharge papers. They framed every disruption as a temporary glitch, a regrettable yet fixable malfunction to be patched by one more stimulus package, one more election, one more leadership summit, one more miracle technology, one more app promising frictionless life. Their energy went into propping up what had been, even as it disintegrated between their fingers, like a building whose facade still looked impressive while the load-bearing beams had already rotted through.

On the other side were those who, often without fanfare and often with a sick heaviness in the chest, accepted a quiet but devastating premise: the old world was gone. Not gone in the literal sense—the buildings still stood, the legal codes were still printed, the logos still blinked from glass towers, the rituals still played on television—but gone at the level that actually mattered: its organizing logic had failed. The assumptions beneath it no longer held. The guarantees it had whispered for generations were no longer backed by anything real.

That acceptance—simple in language, brutal in practice—was the first act of evolution.

Once a person allowed that sentence to settle—this world no longer works the way it promised it would—they could stop hemorrhaging energy trying to revive a system in denial and could finally, painfully, ask the only question that made sense at such a hinge of history:

Given that everything is shifting beneath my feet, who must I become if I intend not merely to survive the slide, but to build on the other side of it.

It was at this point that the Shift Year ceased to be just a global story about markets and institutions and became an intimately personal story about nervous systems, habits, and courage. Systems change through people, not around them; and people, pressed by the pressure of 2026, began to sort themselves—not by declaration, but by response.

Some doubled down on distraction. They went deeper into the anesthetics they already knew—feeds, shows, outrage, gossip, endless chatter about the latest collapse—as if the right combination of noise could drown out the sensation that something foundational was coming apart. Their days blurred into loops of work performed half-heartedly, content consumed ravenously, and denial curated as carefully as an online persona. They were not villains. They were frightened, overclocked humans whose capacity to metabolize reality had been exceeded, and who did what overloaded organisms always do: they numbed.

Others doubled down on aggression. They found a strange comfort in anger, in the rigid simplicity of blame. The chaos of the world gave them an excuse to sharpen every complexity into a moral weapon. They chose enemies with religious fervor—politicians, migrants, elites, the young, the old, the "globalists," the "ignorant"—and hurled their fear outward in the form of certainty. That rage felt like clarity; it was not. It was a different anesthesia, one that replaced helplessness with hostility while leaving understanding untouched.

And then there was a smaller group.

They did not feel superior, enlightened, or "ready" for what was happening. Many of them felt just as exhausted, disillusioned, and afraid as anyone else. They mourned the loss of familiar scripts, resented the unfairness of timing, and grieved privately for the lives they had expected to live. The difference was not that they felt less pain. The difference was what they chose to do with it. Instead of turning away from the discomfort, they turned toward it with a kind of grim curiosity. They let the year teach them, even when the lessons were expensive.

The supply-chain breakdowns taught them that living in total dependence on global systems they did not understand was not modern convenience, but structural vulnerability. So, instead of only complaining when shelves went half empty and shipping delays stretched into months, they began to study how things actually moved—how raw materials became goods, how ports, trucks, and rails interacted, how energy was produced and distributed, how food traveled from soil to table. They took back a measure of agency by shrinking blind dependence and increasing conscious participation, even if it began with something as modest as learning to repair, to grow, to source locally, to see the invisible freight lines that stitched their lives together.

The economic shocks taught them that a single employer or a single income stream, once sold as prudence and stability, had quietly become a point of existential failure. So they learned to create value in multiple ways. Some built small businesses in the margins of their days, on late nights and early mornings when the rest of the world was scrolling. Others turned specialized knowledge into consulting, teaching, or digital products; they began to see their experience not as a résumé line, but as intellectual capital that could be recombined and repurposed. They treated artificial intelligence not as a replacement for their thinking, but as an amplifier of it—a force multiplier that could extend their reach if they learned how to direct it. Instead of asking the fearful question, "Will this take my job," they asked the architectural one, "How do I build something this cannot easily replace, and how do I use it to build faster than I could alone."

The political theater taught them that no party, no leader, no single institution would arrive to rescue them from complexity. So they stopped outsourcing moral judgment to branded structures and reacquired the heavy, adult responsibility to think. They read beyond headlines. They cross-checked narratives that had once been consumed uncritically. They tolerated the discomfort of "I do not know yet" and resisted the cheap thrill of instant outrage. They learned to hold two conflicting data points in mind without collapsing into cynicism or tribal loyalty.

The psychological crash taught them that their minds and bodies were not disposable hardware to be driven into the red zone indefinitely in service of someone else's quarterly targets. They began to treat rest not as a guilty indulgence, but as infrastructure—a non-negotiable component of their capacity to remain clear in a world where clarity had become a scarce resource. They carved out hours where no device had permission to speak to them. They retrained nervous systems that had been conditioned to panic at silence to endure stillness long enough for deeper thought to surface. They remembered hobbies that existed before algorithms. They reintroduced unmonetized play and discovered, to their own surprise, that the richest ideas often emerged precisely in the spaces that could not be tracked, measured, or monetized.

The entertainment pandemic taught them that unlimited access to content did not equal abundance; in many cases, it disguised depletion. So they shifted, sometimes awkwardly and slowly, from pure consumption to creation. They made music instead of only curating it. They wrote instead of scrolling past other people's sentences. They gathered small groups in person, in living rooms and backyards and borrowed spaces, instead of treating connection as something permanently mediated by screens. They did not renounce the digital world; they simply refused to let it collapse the entire spectrum of their existence into a single glowing rectangle.

Each of these adjustments, taken alone, was small—a choice on a Tuesday, a new habit started on a Sunday, a book ordered instead of another subscription. None of them went viral. None of them were trending sounds. No algorithm rewarded them with confetti. But taken across millions of individuals scattered across continents, they did something enormous.

They shifted the locus of agency.

For generations, the dominant story had been that large forces—markets, governments, corporations, platforms—were the primary authors of ordinary lives. Individuals were cast as consumers, voters, employees, users. The verbs that mattered belonged to institutions. In 2026, those forces revealed themselves as powerful but brittle, grand but fallible, vast but strangely confused by the very world they had helped build. The myth of their omnipotence cracked.

The people who understood this stopped waiting for instructions from remote tables. They stopped asking, with a passivity disguised as sophistication, "What are they going to do about this," and began asking the far more dangerous and generative question, "What am I willing to build, even if I begin alone, even if no one is watching, even if the first attempts are small and unimpressive."

These were the Architects.

Architects, in the deepest sense, are not only professionals who draw up plans for visible structures; they are the humans who design frameworks for living. In the ruins and corrections of 2026, Architects began sketching new frameworks in the margins of their ordinary days. New ways of working that did not depend entirely on fragile office hierarchies or single locations, but wove together remote tools, local anchors, and flexible arrangements. New forms of community that were not built solely on shared outrage or shared enemies, but on shared values, mutual support, and clear agreements. New financial models that paired the relative stability of older instruments with the experimental leverage of new ones, balancing risk instead of running from it blindly. New uses of technology that treated human limits not as flaws to be exploited, but as boundaries to be respected and protected.

Some of these Architects operated at visible scale, founding companies, movements, or platforms whose names would one day be written in case studies. Many more worked at smaller scales that would never make the front page—rebuilding a family culture, reweaving a neighborhood, reconceiving a classroom, redesigning a local business, forming digital circles that functioned like micro-civilizations. The scale mattered less than the orientation. Their lives leaned forward. They were building into the future instead of clinging backward into the past.

The Shift Year burned one more truth into the record.

Adaptation is not a fixed personality trait reserved for the naturally "resilient." It is a skill, and like all serious skills, it is trainable, improvable, and, in times of upheaval, non-optional.

The people who seemed "ready" for 2026 were not mysteriously born more capable. They had, often without naming it, spent years practicing mental flexibility—allowing new information to revise old conclusions rather than bouncing off their defenses. They had rehearsed letting go of identities that no longer fit instead of forcing themselves to live inside costumes that had grown too tight. They had started over in small ways—new careers, new cities, new habits—so when life demanded that they start over in larger ways, the sensation was terrifying but not entirely unfamiliar.

That is why the split in 2026 cut so deep. It was not fundamentally about who had the most resources when the year opened. It was about who had the greatest capacity to change their mind about the world and about themselves without collapsing into fragmentation.

Those who could not bear to update their worldview experienced the Shift Year as pure catastrophe. Every correction felt like an assault. Every new emergence felt like an erasure of sacred norms. Every invitation to grow sounded like an accusation that who they had been was inadequate. They clung to the wreckage not because it was safe, but because it was known.

Those who, however reluctantly, allowed their worldview to be revised by evidence experienced 2026 differently. It was still brutal. They still lost. They still grieved. But alongside the grief, they saw openings where others saw only endings. They noticed new needs appearing as old systems failed—needs for guidance, for infrastructure, for repair. They noticed new forms of work emerging where old job titles evaporated. They noticed that as old institutions bled legitimacy, new kinds of leadership—more distributed, more transparent, more accountable—were not only possible, but necessary.

This did not turn them into unshakable optimists. It simply meant they were not paralyzed. They could move, even while afraid. They could decide, even while uncertain.

If you pull back and look at any epoch of upheaval with a historian's patience, you will find the same arc repeating under different costumes. When the Black Death tore through Europe, it did not only annihilate lives; it rewrote land relations, labor markets, and class structures, because survivors were forced to renegotiate everything from scratch. When the Industrial Revolution displaced centuries-old crafts, those who embraced machines and urbanization reshaped production and the very architecture of cities, while those who refused were either crushed or dragged into adaptation later on harsher terms. When the internet arrived, those who learned to build inside its logic reinvented commerce, communication, and culture, while others watched the ground shift beneath established professions.

2026 belongs to that lineage.

Future historians will argue over the exact dates and inflection points; they will debate whether the old world truly ended in one year or whether it had been dying in slow motion for decades. They will annotate graphs of inflation, automation, climate disruption, and conflict; they will highlight treaties signed and institutions restructured. But what will remain hardest to graph—and most decisive for the shape of the century—is what happened inside individual minds and hearts in kitchens, hallways, parked cars, and long, solitary walks at dusk.

Millions of quiet decisions, made without applause:

Decisions to stop trying to squeeze one more season out of a strategy that was visibly dead.

Decisions to begin, however clumsily and anonymously, something genuinely new.

Decisions to question assumptions that had been treated as sacred simply because they were old.

Decisions to cultivate clarity—even when clarity hurt—over the cheaper comfort of self-deception.

Taken together, those decisions turned 2026 from a year of collapse into a year of transition.

To call it merely a crisis is to misunderstand it. A crisis ends when the acute symptoms resolve and the patient returns to baseline. A shift continues, because it is not about the incident; it is about identity. The Shift Year did not merely demand that humanity endure twelve months of pressure and then exhale. It demanded that humanity choose who it intended to be on the far side of pressure, when the dust settled and the new landscape hardened into habit.

For those who chose to stay asleep, the years after 2026 felt like a string of misfortunes: bad luck, bad leaders, bad times. They spoke about earlier decades with aching nostalgia, as if the past were a lost country that cosmic cruelty had barred them from visiting again.

For those who chose to wake up, those same years felt brutal, but strangely clarifying. They remembered 2026 the way a patient remembers the day a difficult diagnosis was finally spoken aloud—not as the moment the illness arrived, but as the moment denial ended, the moment treatment could begin. Painful, yes. But also honest.

They realized that the world they had inherited had already run its course. The world they were building next was not guaranteed by any charter or prophecy. It would exist only if enough people were willing to participate in its construction, to take on the risk of being early to the future instead of comfortably late to the past.

That is the essence of the Shift.

Not a change in calendar, but a change in consciousness.

Not the end of history, but the end of pretending that obsolete habits could solve novel realities.

Not a demand to predict everything, but a demand to see clearly enough to move with intention in a field of uncertainty.

In that sense, the Shift Year was not searching for survivors. Survival can be passive. You can survive by clinging to floating debris. You can survive by hiding in the wreckage of the previous order and letting others decide the shape of what comes next.

What 2026 was searching for were architects.

Men and women who could look at a world colliding with itself and say, with no guarantee of applause, "If everything familiar is cracking, then everything fundamental is open. If the old story is over, then the next one will not write itself. Someone will have to pick up a pen. It might as well be me."

They did not know, in the moment, that they were shaping history. They knew only that living half-awake inside a dying pattern had become intolerable. That continuing to perform normalcy in a world that was visibly abnormal was a slow form of spiritual suffocation. So they chose, in ways large and small, another path.

They chose to become clear, even when clarity cost them old identities.

They chose to become adaptive, even when adaptation felt like humiliation.

They chose to become architects rather than spectators, authors rather than only readers of their era.

The Shift Year did not crown them with titles or medals. It challenged them. It stripped away illusions that had cushioned earlier generations. It burned off excuses that had once sounded plausible. It placed them in a world where every decision—what to learn, who to trust, where to build, what to ignore—mattered a little more because the script had been thrown out.

And in that unscripted space, under pressure that would have crushed other ages into pure despair, the next era quietly began.

EPILOGUE

The Flashlight

History books like clean endings. They fence off eras with dates and names and headlines, as if the world pivots when a signature dries on a treaty or a countdown hits zero on a broadcast. They like to pretend that history moves in straight lines and tidy chapters, that an empire collapses on a Tuesday and a new age begins on a Wednesday, all properly labeled for future reference.

Reality is less obedient than that.

It shifts like a fault line—pressure building in silence, tiny slips no one notices, then sudden breaks and long aftershocks. It changes slowly, then violently, then slowly again, in waves that do not care what year the calendar says or what the headline of the day happens to be.

And yet, every so often, there is a corridor of years that refuses to stay quiet. A narrow stretch that historians will circle in red a generation from now and say, "That was it. That is where the old story exhausted itself, and the new one insisted on being born."

For our era, that corridor runs from 2026 to 2030.

If you open the calendar app on most phones and scroll forward, you can see an accidental metaphor hiding in the software. The coming years are preloaded with holidays and observances, little digital markers telling you which days society has agreed to treat as sacred or significant. Days of memory. Days of rest. Days of sanctioned celebration.

Then you arrive at 2030.

On many devices, the familiar list thins out or disappears altogether. No flags. No labels. Blank squares. An official future with no prewritten meaning.

Technically, it is a quirk of programming. Symbolically, it is a mirror.

The world behind you is crowded with someone else's meanings—old rituals, old loyalties, old definitions of success and safety and "normal." The stretch in front of you is not. The next configuration has not been decided yet. The script is unresolved.

2026 is the threshold into that unresolved space. 2030 is the far edge of it. Between them lies the hinge—those four years when the world as it used to operate finally hit its limit, and a different way of living, building, and leading stopped being optional and started being required.

That corridor will not automatically produce a better world. It is not a prophecy. It is a test. It is only guaranteed to expose the world we have already built and the people we have already become.

To walk through it and come out more alive, humanity will have to do the one thing it has been avoiding for a very long time:

Raise its frequency.

Raise its capacity.

Not as a hashtag. Not as a vague affirmation. In the most concrete sense possible.

Raising frequency means raising the level at which you perceive and respond. It means refusing to live permanently at the emotional altitude of comment sections and panic headlines. It means trading reflex for reflection, numbness for awareness, consumption for creation. It is the difference between being dragged by the story and stepping back far enough to see who is writing it—and why.

Raising capacity means strengthening what your mind, body, and spirit can hold without splitting. It means building nervous systems that can sit with complexity without dissolving into either denial or hysteria. It means training yourself to feel fear without becoming its employee. To receive new information without instantly retreating into old beliefs. To stay with uncomfortable truth without sprinting to the nearest distraction.

You cannot legislate those upgrades. You cannot pass a bill that says, "From this day forward, everyone will be clear, awake, and honest with themselves." No parliament can do that. No boardroom can do that. No algorithm will do it for you.

It is cultivated one human at a time. One decision at a time. One quiet refusal to drop back into sleep.

That is where the Flashlight enters.

There comes a moment in every collapsing order when someone—not a politician, not a celebrity, not a savior in the movie sense—steps forward quietly with a single beam of clarity cutting through the dark.

They do not look like the old kind of leader. They do not spend their days crafting soundbites or measuring their impact in followers. They rarely fit the resume that institutions have been trained to respect. They move differently. They see differently.

They carry sight.

Not omniscience. Not a perfect forecast of every market, every election, every war. They carry something simpler and more subversive: the willingness to look directly at reality without flinching, even when that reality indicts everything they were taught to trust.

They see the rubble and the blueprint at the same time.

They see the danger and the doorway in the same frame.

They see the systems shaking and the people being crushed inside them, and they refuse to pretend it is fine.

The Flashlight does not appear out of nowhere. It is not a mystical stranger dropping in from a different dimension. It is a human being that the last decade has been grinding, tempering, humiliating, and sharpening—just like everyone else—except for one crucial difference:

Where most people turned away from the friction, they turned toward it.

Where most people clung harder to old identities, they allowed themselves to molt.

Where most people chased comfort until comfort became chains, they let discomfort change them.

They lived through the same years you did.

They watched 2017–2024 set the stage, even if they could not yet name what they were feeling. They saw trust leak quietly out of institutions. They watched social media evolve from novelty to necessity to narcotic. They watched "once-in-a-lifetime" disruptions arrive every year. They lived through the slow boil of anxiety, the background hum of "this cannot be how life is supposed to feel," and they stopped gaslighting themselves about it.

They committed, not to being perfect, but to being honest. To raising their own frequency in a low-frequency environment. To increasing their own capacity in a time when the default response was to shrink.

Because they did, the world around them changed tone.

They saw war in the machine—code attacking code, narratives attacking minds—and also saw the possibility of building new networks that were not designed purely for extraction and manipulation.

They saw money get rewritten—fiat eroding, crypto rising and crashing, central banks digitizing currencies—and also saw the chance to design new forms of value that did not require total dependence on brittle intermediaries.

They saw surveillance metastasize—eyes everywhere, microphones everywhere, data trails on everything—and also saw the invitation to become the kind of human who cannot be cheaply steered even when being constantly watched.

They saw the psychological crash—burnout, numbness, quiet desperation—and also saw the doorway to rebuild inner lives on something deeper than performance and dopamine.

They saw the entertainment pandemic—people bingeing themselves into paralysis—and also felt the hunger for stories that heal, frameworks that strengthen, spaces that do not trade clarity for clicks.

They saw a people divided—tribes screaming at tribes, leaders monetizing hatred—and also sensed, underneath the noise, how many were secretly starving for actual connection.

They saw the echoes of old empires—overextended, overentertained, overconfident, internally hollow—and also saw what every collapse has always made possible: a reset that clears space for something wiser, leaner, braver to be built.

They saw crisis breed innovators and Observers begin to stand up in the middle of the chaos. They watched the Shift Year separate sleepers from the awake, spectators from Architects. They recognized themselves in that separation and made a decision:

If everything is going to change, someone is going to decide what it changes into.

I refuse to leave that decision entirely to the ones who broke it.

That is the moment a person becomes a Flashlight.

But before we talk about what they build, we need to peel back a layer that most books, most leaders, most commentators are still too polite to touch.

Because it is not only systems that are being exposed. It is people. It is you—if you insist on staying who you were in a world that cannot survive who it has been.

All of you who refused to wake up.

All of you who clung to the old ways even as they cracked in your hands.

All of you who hid behind titles and gatekeeping and polished statements.

All of you who mistook your scar tissue for wisdom and your insecurity for authority.

You are being lit up.

You executives who sat in glass offices in 2025 and 2026, watching AI demos you did not understand, nodded along in public and mocked them in private, then quietly ordered your teams to extract more from the same tired workforce instead of redesigning the way work is done—you are visible now.

You politicians who learned that outrage was the cheapest path to re-election, who fed division because it kept you funded, who treated war and policy like pieces on a board and human beings like abstractions—you are visible now.

You religious leaders who wrapped your fear of change in doctrine, who shut down questions because they threatened your control, who used spiritual language to keep people small and dependent instead of clear and empowered—you are visible now.

You media architects who optimized your platforms for engagement at any cost, who knew exactly what panic and anger were doing to the public psyche and pressed "publish" anyway, night after night—you are visible now.

You gatekeepers in every industry who hoarded access, who placed yourselves at the bottlenecks of opportunity, who pretended to be guardians of quality when in truth you were guardians of your own status—you are visible now.

The Flashlight does not expose you with scandal headlines or cancel campaigns. That is theater, and theater is part of the problem. The Flashlight exposes you by making your patterns impossible to hide in the light of a raised collective awareness.

Because once enough people learn to see, manipulation looks cheap.

Once enough people reclaim their agency, gatekeeping looks small.

Once enough people raise their frequency, old leaders who refuse to grow look like exactly what they are: scared.

Scared of being irrelevant.

Scared of being outgrown.

Scared of being seen without the costumes of their roles.

You can feel it in rooms where old power still tries to operate the way it did in 2010. The jokes no one laughs at anymore. The talking points that ring hollow. The strategies that were designed for a distracted population and now land on people who are starting to read the fine print.

The Flashlight does not humiliate you. It gives you a choice you can no longer pretend you were not offered:

Evolve or be bypassed.

Grow or be archived.

Drop the performance and do the work of becoming real—or watch other hands pick up the tools of the future while you complain about "how things used to be."

The same light that exposes their insecurity is the light that exposes yours.

All of you who chose, year after year, to anesthetize instead of awaken—this light lands on you too.

All of you who spent the years between 2017 and 2026 perfecting your escape routes—scrolling yourself to sleep, arguing in comment sections, bingeing other people's lives while quietly abandoning your own—this light lands on you.

All of you who felt the war in the machine, the eyes everywhere, the money shifting, the psychological weight, the entertainment addiction, the division, the cracks in the empire—and told yourself, "This is just how things are now, there's nothing I can do, might as well distract myself"—this light lands on you.

It is not a light of condemnation. It is a light without anesthesia.

It reveals that your numbness has a cost.

It reveals that your apathy is not neutral.

It reveals that clinging to old habits in a collapsing world is not safety. It is slow self-erasure.

The Flashlight shines on all of that and says, without theatrics:

This is what your choices are building.

This is what your avoidance is funding.

This is the world your passivity is voting for.

And then it turns, just as clearly, to the smaller group—the Observers, the innovators, the Architects, the ones who let the Shift Year teach them instead of break them—and it shows them something different:

This is what your courage is opening.

This is what your clarity is carving out.

This is the world your quiet discipline is already shaping.

All the chapters before this one have been describing the terrain.

War in the Machine.

Supply chains snapping like overused tendons.

The rise of AI as both threat and leverage.

Eyes Everywhere.

The Psychological Crash.

Money Rewritten.

Escapism and the Entertainment Pandemic.

A People Divided.

Echoes of Old Empires.

Crisis breeding Innovators.

The Observer.

The Shift Year and the Rise of Architects.

You have walked through each of those arc-lines, seeing how they braid together into a single moment: a world that has outrun its old operating system and is now glitching in plain sight.

This epilogue is not about the systems anymore. It is about you.

Not you as a demographic segment, not you as a target audience, not you as a "user" in somebody's report. You: the one nervous system you actually inhabit. The one story you can actually write from the inside.

When you close this book, nothing external instantly calms down.

The feeds will still be loud.

The markets will still be erratic.

The headlines will still weaponize your fear if you let them.

The platforms will still compete for your attention like predators circling the same signal.

What changes is not the storm. What changes is the kind of captain you choose to be in your own vessel.

You can drift into 2030 on autopilot, letting your devices decide your rituals, letting your notifications decide your priorities, letting your exhaustion decide your limits, letting your fear decide your identity.

Or you can step into 2030 as what this entire book has been trying to name inside you:

A Flashlight.

Someone who has chosen to raise their frequency above the default setting of this age.

Someone who has practiced awareness enough that manipulation hits and echoes instead of sticking and sinking. Someone who has stretched their capacity enough that every new shock does not shatter them back to zero. Someone who remembers that the empty squares on that digital calendar are not a glitch.

They are an invitation.

An invitation to mark new days as sacred—days where you choose depth over distraction, contribution over consumption, presence over performance.

An invitation to design new rituals that support growth instead of numbing.

An invitation to honor not just the survival of old structures, but the evolution of human consciousness itself.

If enough people accept that invitation, the world that emerges on the far side of this corridor will not be utopia. It will still be messy, because human beings are messy. But it will be less built on denial and more on reality. Less optimized for a shrinking elite and more capable of holding the many. Less reliant on gatekeepers and more animated by Architects who remember where they came from.

And that shift will not be granted by charity from the top. It will be forced into being by clarity from within.

Because when people see, truly see, they become very difficult to rule through confusion.

When enough people refuse to match the frequency of chaos, chaos loses half its leverage.

When enough people refuse to stay small in order to keep others comfortable, entire hierarchies start to wobble.

That is why this era feels so intense. It is not just the systems shaking. It is identity itself being asked to upgrade or dissolve.

There comes a moment in every collapsing world

when someone

not a politician,

not a celebrity,

not a savior

steps forward quietly with a single beam of clarity

cutting through the dark.

Not to save the world.

Not to fix everything.

Not to calm the panic.

But simply to see.

To see without distortion.

To see without fear.

To see without noise.

To see without the blindness of comfort or ego.

That someone is the Flashlight.

The Flashlight is not a hero. They are a perspective.

A way of thinking.

A way of being.

A way of standing when everything else is shaking.

The Flashlight is the person who understands that the world may fall apart, but awareness does not.

Systems collapse. Clarity doesn't.

Empires crumble. Perception doesn't.

People panic. Consciousness doesn't.

The Flashlight survives because the Flashlight sees.

The year 2026 did not choose who would rise. It revealed them.

It revealed the ones who refused to drown in noise.

Revealed the ones who chose introspection over distraction.

Revealed the ones who sharpened instead of shattered.

Revealed the ones who learned instead of reacted.

Revealed the ones who did not hide from chaos, but illuminated it.

The Flashlight was not the one untouched by the collision. They were the one transformed by it.

Because transformation is not something the world gifts you as compensation for suffering.

Transformation is something you claim by refusing to waste your suffering.

And here is the truth almost no one will say out loud in a world built on comfort:

Most people will never choose to become the Flashlight.

Most will cling to entertainment like oxygen.

Most will attach their identity to outrage and call it integrity.

Most will scroll themselves numb and call it staying informed.

Most will repeat opinions handed to them and call it thinking.

Most will hug nostalgia tight while the future walks right past them.

Most will fear evolution more than they fear collapse.

But not everyone.

Not you.

If you have made it this far, if this language kept tugging at something under your ribs instead of just skimming your eyes, it is because a part of you was already awake before this book ever found your hands. This did not create the signal. It named it.

You were not looking for a prophecy.

You were looking for confirmation.

Confirmation that the world has felt off for a reason.

Confirmation that you were not crazy to feel the ground shift years before anyone wanted to talk about it.

Confirmation that your restlessness was not immaturity, but early detection.

Confirmation that you were not built merely to survive someone else's collapse, but to participate in a different construction.

Confirmation that you were born into this window of history on purpose, even if you never know the full extent of that purpose.

Confirmation that you are the Flashlight.

This is not about destiny descending from the sky. It is about decision.

You decide whether you rise or numb out.

You decide whether you adapt or calcify.

You decide whether you see or stay blind.

You decide whether you build or complain.

You decide whether you lead from the inside or follow whatever is loudest on the outside.

You decide whether you walk into the next era with clarity or cling to the last one out of fear.

And if you choose clarity, you will not need to announce yourself as a leader.

In a world that shakes, the steady become landmarks.

What comes after 2026 is not primarily destruction.

It is construction.

New systems.

New leaders.

New creators.

New innovators.

New cultures.

New mindsets.

New foundations.

New structures of power and possibility.

Everything is open.

Everything is contested.

Everything is available to the ones who can see.

The world will not return to what it was. It will become what we allow it to become.

So carry the flashlight.

Sharpen your mind.

Guard your attention.

Raise your frequency.

Stretch your capacity.

Stay awake.

S aware.

Stay intentional.

Stay unshaken.

Walk forward with your eyes wide open into a world that is raw and changing and unstable and, precisely because of that, overflowing with leverage for those willing to build with clean hands.

Because the future does not belong to the loud, the angry, the comfortable, or the distracted.

The future belongs to the aware.

To the adaptive.

To the bold.

To the clear.

To the conscious.

To the ones who learned how to see when everyone else forgot how.

The future belongs to the Flashlight.

And if you are reading this, that means it belongs to you.

The End

You will live in the world your clarity and awareness creates.

Observe wisely.